THE
MANUAL

THE MANUAL

TRIVIA

TESTOSTERONE

TALES OF
 BADASSERY

RAW MEAT

FINE WHISKEY

COLD TRUTH

KEITH RIEGERT
SAM KAPLAN

Text Copyright © 2013 Keith Riegert and Sam Kaplan. Design Copyright © 2013 Ulysses Press and its licensors. All rights reserved under International and Pan-American Copyright Conventions.

Published by:
Kingfisher Press

Managing Editor: Claire Chun
Editor: Jessica Benner
Proofreader: Elyce Berrigan-Dunlop
Design and layout: Jake Flaherty
Cover illustration by Robert Emil Schulz is from the collection of Richard Oberg and is used with the permission of Mr. Oberg and the artist's son, Robert Schulz

Image Credits: Unless noted, images sourced from shutterstock.com.

Introduction: man with rifle © Antonio Abrigiani. Blood, Sweat, and Tyranny: Roman warrior © Antonio Abrigiani; Bear hunting © Antonio Abrigiani; Sniper rifle © igorlale; Samurai © Antonio Abrigiani; Seppuku © Antonio Abrigiani; Grenade © SS1001; World map © Volina; Nuke symbol © gigibgm. Meat: Moose © Hein Nouwens; Mammoth © Denis Barbulat; Snake head © Morphart Creation; Parts of a cow © Morphart Creation; Steak logo © Squarelogo; Parts of a pig © Antonio Abrigiani; Parts of a chicken © Antonio Abrigiani. Drinking with Hemingway: Bourbon bottle © RetroClipArt; Map of beer © Aleksandar Mijatovic; Cigar © AKaiser. Boxing: Boxing © Antonio Abrigiani. Your Body Is Your Temple of Doom: Skull © Anteromite; Tapeworm © Morphart Creation; Scabies © Morphart Creation; Wolfman © Antonio Abrigiani. The Sea: Squid and whale © Pika; Parts of boat © Aleksei Makarov; Raft © Antonio Abrigiani; Canoe © Nicku; Kayak © Denis Barbulat; Galley © Antonio Abrigiani; Viking ship © Denis Barbulat; Clipper ship © Regien Paassen; Steamboat © Hein Nouwens; Submarine © Tshooter; Polynesia triangle © StasysEidieJus; Tuna © Morphart Creation; Haddock © Hein Nouwens; Ika © Pika; Fugu © Pio3; Unagi © Hein Nouwens; Saba © Morphart Creation; Sake © Morphart Creation; Tobiko © Hein Nouwens; Tako © Morphart Creation; Uni © Hein Nouwens. Masculaneous: Masked man © Antonio Abrigiani; Opium den © Antonio Abrigiani; Map of Sicily © Antonio Abrigiani; Bat man © Hein Nouwens. Appendix: Skull on wall © Corepics VOF; Dinosaur © Linda Bucklin; Plaque behind dinoasur © RaidenV; Ram head © Joppo; Background edge © Euroshot

IMPORTANT NOTE TO READERS: Trademarks of businesses and food brands mentioned in this book are used for informational purposes only. No sponsorship or endorsement by, or affiliation with, the trademark owners is claimed or suggested by the author or publisher.

CONTENTS

Introduction	**1**
Blood, Sweat, and Tyranny	**5**
Meat	**55**
Drinking with Hemingway	**81**
Boxing	**117**
Your Body Is Your Temple of Doom	**141**
The Sea	**171**
Masculaneous	**231**
Appendix	**255**
Selected Bibliography	**256**
About the Authors	**259**

Introduction

"Damn fine day to be wearing bear skins."

 THE MANual

> *"A man who lives fully is prepared to die at any time."*
> –Mark Twain

Take pride in your manliness. On average, you are taller (around six inches) bigger (by about fifteen percent), stronger and significantly more hairy than our counterpart sex. Societal norms allow you to forgo painting your face with makeup (save for bowl games), shaving your forest-like legs and chin and refraining from unleashing the full volume of your flatulence.

But achieving this level of masculinity is no walk in the park. It takes years of study, practice and broken bones. But for us mushy twenty-first century lads living in the Western World, we've managed to sign up for a pretty sweet progression from pimply boyhood into the respectful post of the gentleman.

Chances are, as you stumbled awkwardly through puberty, there weren't many hardcore rites of passage you had to endure. Maybe you had to get your braces tightened at the orthodontist. Perhaps your mom yelled at you while you were learning to drive. You probably got rejected and it really hurt. Boo-shut-the-hell-up-hoo.

In other parts of the world, the transition from boyhood to man-dom is really physically painful. For the Satere-Mawe Tribe of the Amazon, becoming a man means sticking your hands in gloves filled with bullet ants, a tropical insect aptly named for stings that feel like you're being shot with a gun, and smiling as your flesh burns.

The soon-to-be men of Pentecost Island in the South Pacific shed their childish fears by bungee jumping off a rickety plat-

Introduction

form using rigid vines instead of synthetic chords. The closer to the ground they get, the more respect. A cracked skull is basically the mark of the alpha male.

Speaking of cracking your brain open, if you were raised with the Algonquin Indians of Canada, your journey into manhood would have entailed being left in the northern forest alone after taking a hallucinogen 100 times stronger than LSD. The point of which was to help you find your inner man by forgetting your childhood and, occasionally, who you were altogether.

We're not going to tell you to do any of that. Although, if you do, we'd love to hear about it. Instead, all you have to do is read this book and put some deep thought into your own masculinity.

Sit back on your porcelain throne, relax and expand your knowledge of everything. Whether you're heading to into the boxing ring, the frontlines of battle or the Glenlivet distillery, there are topics you should be able to speak to and questions you should be able to answer.

- How do I properly grill a steak?
- Can I survive a hand grenade attack?
- What's the difference between a KO and TKO?
- How do I choose a proper cigar?
- What's the difference between "neat" and "straight up"?

The answers await, brother. Let's stop wasting time. Welcome to *The MANual*. Good luck and we'll see you on the other side.

Blood, Sweat, and Tyranny

Warriors, Empires, and Death

TEN WARRIORS WHO PUT THE "AWE" IN AWESOME

Since the beginning of history, men have sought out eternal glory on the field of battle. And their names actually do live on in eternal glory: from Achilles, Genghis Khan, and Scipio Africanus to Washington, Grant, and Nimitz, these men are never forgotten. Here are some warriors that should appear in more textbooks, movies, and your nightmares.

Mad Jack and His Bagpipes

When Lt. Colonel "Mad" Jack Churchill marched on his first Nazi garrison in 1941, he carried just two weapons: a longbow and a broadsword. A couple years later, he led a commando charge in Yugoslavia playing bagpipes the entire time. Of the forty commandos that made the charge, Mad Jack and his bagpipes were the only survivors. For his years of valor and for being a huge badass and the only soldier in all of WWII to kill an enemy fighter with a longbow, he was awarded the Distinguished Service Order.

So Much Depends on the White Feather in the Green Forest

Ninety-three. That was the staggering confirmed body count that Marine scout sniper Carlos Hathcock managed to rack up during the Vietnam War. Not only was Hathcock a crack

BLOOD, SWEAT, AND TYRANNY

shot and ridiculously good at hiding, he also had the unbelievable balls to always wear an unmistakable white feather in his bush hat during combat, which for a jungle sniper seems the equivalent of wearing a flashing neon target on the side of his head. His trademark look earned him the name White Feather from the Viet Cong and a bounty on the head behind the feather that today would be worth about $200,000.

Hathcock was such a thorn in the Viet Cong's side (and head, heart, and various vital organs) that entire squads of enemy snipers were sent out to track him. In one torn-from-a-Hollywood-script account, Hathcock went mano a mano in a jungle gully with a highly talented North Vietnamese sniper. With both snipers quietly stalking one another from either end of the ravine, Hathcock caught sight of an unnatural glint of light and, gambling, took a shot right at it. The glint turned out to be the scope of the Vietnamese rifle, which, coincidentally had been zeroed in on Hathcock's face. Unfor-

WHITE DEATH

While Carlos Hathcock was one hell of a sniper, almost nobody compares to the little-known Finnish sharpshooter, Simo Häyhä. Nicknamed White Death by the opposing Russian forces during the Winter War of 1939–1940, Häyhä managed an amazing feat unmatched to this day: he killed 505 enemy combatants, the most sniper kills in history. And he did it in less than 100 days. In the dead of winter. Using a rifle with no telescopic sight.

> Rome's Colosseum set the stage for the slaughter of
> 500,000 people and over 1,000,000 animals.

tunately for the guy behind the scope, Hathcock's shot was clean and true—perfectly passing through the glass scope and coming to rest in the man's brain.

A Viking with a Bone to Pick

Descended from a long line of Viking warlord badasses (even his dad's name is intimidating: Ragnar Lodbrok), Ivar the Boneless was a Viking to be reckoned with. Ivar's reign of supreme asswhoopery began in 865 when he and his brothers led an army of Norse berserkers against East Anglia in England to avenge their father's capture and assassination. The East Anglians were so petrified of Ivar and his ragtag team of rabid Viking warmongers that, instead of fighting, they gave them horses and shelter for the winter. The next year, Ivar led his army north, where they sacked York and installed a puppet king.

For perhaps his most dangerous feat, Ivar the Boneless became the first invader in the history of ever to successfully capture the fortress of Dumbarton in the Kingdom of Strathclyde. Sure, it sounds like something out of a bad fantasy novel, but the fortress was one of England's most secure territorial strongholds at the time.

BLOOD, SWEAT, AND TYRANNY

What's clear is about Ivar the Boneless is that he was an incredible warrior and savvy commander. What's not clear is why he had such a strange nickname. Ivar's fans say it was because of an almost inhuman physical flexibility, while detractors claim he was impotent or infertile. Our favorite theory, however, is that the man had a brilliant mind but brittle, useless bones, and commanded his armies while riding atop a shield carried by his troops.

A Thousand Ways to Kill

There are countless ways to kill, and Yue Fei wanted to master them all. A Renaissance man of the Chinese military arts, Yui Fei is considered one of the greatest military minds of all

ALL THE MAGICAL COLORS OF BLOOD

The term "berserk" can be traced back to a fabled group of fearless Norse warriors called berserkers, who would work themselves into a nearly uncontrollable, rage-filled frenzy just before battle. So intense was their mania that they were apparently immune to pain. Impaled by spear? A splinter. Sliced by scion? A paper cut. Burned by fire? It'll turn into a tan.

Theorists offer various explanations of how berserkers achieved such heightened levels of savagery, but the best regarded theory is that they were hardcore tweakers who would prepare for battle by getting high out of their minds on one of the world's most potent natural hallucinogens: psilocybin "magic" mushrooms.

time. Strong as an ox, Yue Fei could wield the biggest bows with either hand, he could spar with a spear, and he invented several combat styles, including Eagle Claw and Xingyi boxing. And as if those talents weren't enough? Fei could also bore you to death with his poetry.

Fei's is a rags-to-riches underdog story about loyalty, revenge, and creative bloodshed. He rose through the ranks of the Song army when China was split into three feuding factions, the most powerful of which were Fei's Song and the back-stabbing nomadic Jin to the north. Around 1125, the Jin broke an alliance with the Song, and Fei went absolutely nuts, storming up north leading a ragtag army of 800 against a massive Jin force 50,000 strong. Eventually Fei's overmatched crew was forced to retreat.

But Fei redoubled his efforts and began dreaming of various ways to destroy his sworn enemy. He began an intense and bloody campaign to consolidate the massive Song army, killing any traitor, rebel, or rabble-rouser he deemed worthy of death. Once he had control of all militia within Song strongholds, he proceeded once again up north, winning bloody battle after bloody battle and recapturing Song territory from those meddlesome Jin punks. Fei had momentum, military brilliance, and a fiercely loyal army: he was poised to expand the Song Empire ever northward.

Unfortunately, there was a growing faction of peace-loving hippies in the Song government who not only wanted to end the war, but who thought the best way to create peace was

BLOOD, SWEAT, AND TYRANNY

to kill their former enemy's biggest enemy. They sarcastically thanked Fei for all his help, shoved him in a prison, and in 1142 executed their most celebrated and beloved military general.

The Accidental Warrior

For some brave soldiers who fought in World War II, the war metaphorically and emotionally never ended. For Lt. Hiroo Onoda, it literally almost didn't. In 1942, young Onoda joined the Imperial Army of Japan and by 1944 was tasked with waging covert guerilla warfare on the remote Philippine island of Lubang. Onoda and a very small cell of operatives ended up left behind in the high jungles as the island was overrun by Allied forces shortly before the war came to a dramatic end with the unconditional surrender of Japan.

Unfortunately, Onoda never got that final, important message. Despite numerous leaflets dropped by American planes proclaiming the end of combat, Onoda wouldn't buy that Japan had lost. So he continued to hide in the jungle, subsisting primarily on coconuts and tropical fruit, still waging war on the Allied forces…for twenty-nine years. Finally, on March 9, 1974, the Japanese government was forced to send his orig-

---

Britain owns the distinction of having fought in both history's shortest war (thirty-eight minutes vs. Zanzibar) and its longest (116 years vs. France).

inal commanding officer to Lubang to officially request his surrender, which he reluctantly gave.

Save the Worm for Ingacio

For many twenty-first-century American gringos, Cinco de Mayo conjures up images of guacamole, empty Corona bottles, tequila, puking in a Chevy's sombrero, and some vague connection to Mexico's independence. But in 1862, the date stood for one of the most awe-inspiring underdog victories of all time. That's because on the original Cinco de Mayo, the French Army, being owed a crap-load of money by the government of Mexico, found out just how hard it can be to collect on a loan. On their way to sack Mexico City, the French arrived in the town of Puebla where they met a scrappy Mexican force led by the brilliant commander Ignacio Zaragoza Seguín.

Most of Seguín's troops, whose numbers amounted to about half those of the French, were armed with nothing more than rusty machetes and the steely reserve of men raised on fermented cactus. The French laughed, loaded their pristine rifles and muskets, and were brutally slaughtered by the knife-wielding Mexicans. Having your army's ass kicked by a bunch of guys hacking at you with tetanus-laden machetes

> "They couldn't hit an elephant from this distance."
> —*The unfortunate last words of General John Sedgwick, killed by a Confederate sniper during the American Civil War*

did not inspire a lot of confidence from the French homeland and that particular fifth of May helped, eventually, in convincing the French to abandon their colonial ambitions and head home.

An Economy of Blood

The history of New Zealand is coated in guts, gore, face tattoos, severed heads, and intense tribal warfare. Until Europeans introduced potatoes and muskets to the Maori, however, men were too busy farming and doing other domestic chores to do what they really wanted to do, which was, apparently, kill each other all the time. Potatoes, you see, were so easy to farm that the men entrusted their women and slaves to do the job, freeing the Maori men to take their talents to the battlefield.

But this story is not just about potatoes, it's also about guns. Despite 150 years of contact with Europeans, Maoris continued to engage in battle using traditional weapons, including staffs, clubs, and bladed weapons made of wood or whalebone. But one day in 1807, a visionary named Hongi Hika, an emerging war leader of the Ngāpuhi iwi (tribe), had an epiphany that muskets were the weapon of the future. He helped lead his iwi in a battle against their rivals, the Ngāti Whātua iwi, but the Ngāpuhi were besieged as they reloaded their muskets.

Hika was not to be discouraged; he understood the raw, awesome power of the musket and just knew that they were superior to wooden clubs and blades. So in a landmark deal, he traded some prime New Zealand real estate to an adventurer named Charles de Thierry in exchange for no fewer than 500 muskets. He promptly raised an army and between 1806 and 1828 he laid brutal, deadly waste to most of northern New Zealand and basically made himself overlord of the Maori. These skirmishes are now known as the Musket Wars.

But Hika wasn't entirely westernized. He was married to a clairvoyant blind lady and her sister and he still enjoyed chopping off the heads of his slain enemies. Around this time, dried human noggins were a popular novelty item throughout Europe, and Hika realized the lucrative potential of warfare. Thus began a sort of ironic cycle of bloodshed and capitalism: he lopped off more heads in order to buy more weapons, and he bought more weapons in order to acquire more heads.

By the mid-1820s, however, the other Maori tribes had realized the devastating power of the musket and began to procure some for themselves. A bullet pierced Hika's chest in 1827 and, in one of the most badass deaths on record, he encouraged his men to gather around and listen to the poetic whispers of the wind as it whistled in and then out of his lungs.

The Ungentlemanly Gentleman

One of the Second World War's greatest guerilla warriors was the French Count Robert Jean Marie de La Rochefoucauld. Young Robert began his passionate Nazi-killing crusade at the tender age of sixteen after the Germans abducted and killed his father, Olivier de La Rochefoucauld. In seeking vengeance, Robert joined the French resistance movement, which quickly got him put on the Germans' this-guy-needs-to-die list, forcing him to flee first to Paris and then to Spain.

It was here that Rochefoucauld performed his first brilliant act of deceit when, after being sent to a Spanish prison camp, he dropped his French accent and convinced his captors that he was actually a limey Brit, affording him a trip to the British Embassy to get everything straightened out.

The Brits at the embassy were so thoroughly impressed with his acting skills they enlisted him in the most notorious WWII espionage outfit, the British Special Operations Executive, otherwise known as the Ministry of Ungentlemanly Warfare.

After a few months of intensive training in London, he was parachuted into France, where he proceeded to wreak havoc—by doing things like blowing up a factory using explosive-laden loaves of bread. His Nazi-killing did not go unnoticed. Despite being captured and sentenced to death

> "In my dreams I hear again the crash of guns, the rattle of musketry, the strange, mournful mutter of the battlefield. But in the evening of my memory always I come back to West Point. Always there echoes and re-echoes: Duty, Honor, Country."
>
> —US General (and general badass) Douglas MacArthur

twice by the Nazis, Rochefoucald used his intense bloodlust and natural skills to escape. The first time, he jumped out of the back of the truck transporting him to his execution, dodged some machine gun fire, stole a Nazi limo, and made his way back to Paris. The second time, he faked a seizure while in prison and dispatched the responding guard with the jagged leg he had snapped off a table. He then walked around the detention center, shooting Nazi guards before stealing a nun's habit and making his escape.

Good Morning, Vietnam

You know that one savage firefight sequence in every amazing action movie that you absolutely love but think is so far from reality? Well, let Master Sergeant Roy P. Benavidez restore your faith in all that is awesome and explosive.

On the morning of May 2, 1968, Sgt. Benavidez found himself monitoring the combat radio at Forward Operating Base Loc Ninh, just north of Saigon. A Special Forces unit of twelve men, tasked with gathering intelligence on a possible nearby buildup of North Vietnamese Army troops, had just been dropped into the jungle a little ways from the sarge. Well, uncover a slight buildup they did, and the twelve-man

> The first recorded use of chemical warfare dates back to the fifth century BC, when the Spartans used sulfur bombs to suffocate the Athenians during the Peloponnesian War.

BLOOD, SWEAT, AND TYRANNY

unit found themselves pinned down by about 1,000 well-armed North Vietnamese.

After listening in horror as three helicopters failed to reach the pinned team, Sgt. Benavidez took action. He hopped on a returning chopper and headed toward the landing zone, which was now awash in a sea of hot lead. Trying to avoid the firefight, the helicopter dropped Sgt. Benavidez 75 yards from the Special Forces team. During his 250-foot dash, Sgt. Benavidez (who had conveniently forgotten his rifle in the confusion of the moment) was shot four times. But he never stopped running. When he reached the crippled team, he immediately set about carrying and dragging all the living soldiers back to the waiting chopper.

With all the soldiers accounted for, and being a thorough military man with little regard for his own personal safety, Sgt. Benavidez then ran the 250 bullet-laced feet back to the dead body of the team leader in order to retrieve any classified documents that might be laying around. At which point he was shot in the stomach, had a grenade blow up next to his back, and then watched the helicopter with all the soldiers he'd just rescued crash back to earth.

Did he cry? No. Where any normal superhuman being would have given up, Sgt. Benavidez was just getting started. The sarge got up, tucked his organs back into his shirt, ran back to the downed chopper, gathered up whatever souls in the wreckage were still breathing, and positioned them in a defensive perimeter until another helicopter could arrive. He

THE MANual

then cranked up the radio, called in some air strikes, and ran around handing out water and ammo to the wounded soldiers (what, no moist towelettes?). Oh, and then he got shot again.

When the extraction helicopter finally arrived, Sgt. Benavidez dispatched a couple final North Vietnamese soldiers, was pulled on board, and promptly blacked out. But not before spitting in the face of a doctor who mistakenly declared him dead. By the time he was rescued, Sgt. Benavidez had acquired thirty-seven new holes in his body and had saved the lives of eight men. For his actions, he was awarded the Medal of Honor and two ounces of brand new blood.

Cold, Naked Revenge

During the 1700s, the Catawba Indians (of present day North and South Carolina) were in a near-constant state of warfare with their neighbors, the Iroquois Seneca. The blood feud between the tribes ran deep and fierce. So fierce, in fact, that when a Seneca raiding party happened upon a lone Catawba warrior, a mini war broke out on the spot.

During the skirmish, the remarkably skilled Catawba warrior managed to slaughter seven Seneca before being captured, viciously stripped, and tortured. With their captive now secure, the Seneca went about exacting revenge for their seven

> "It's better to die on your feet than live on your knees."
>
> —Emiliano Zapata, Mexican revolutionary
> and epic mustache-haver

fallen friends, marching the naked Catawba warrior back to their village to be burned alive. It's just about here that things went all wrong for the Seneca.

As they paraded the naked warrior around their camp and down to the adjacent river to be toasted and roasted, the Catawba warrior broke free, dove into the river and skinny-dipped across in just one breath. When he reached the other side of the river, the warrior taunted the Seneca by slapping his bare ass (in the midst of rifle fire) before taking off on foot at breakneck speeds presumably only possible when running ass-naked to save your life. The Catawba warrior ran so fast and so far that he ended up with a huge lead over his pissed-off pursuers.

After two days, a group of five Seneca unknowingly caught up to the hiding nude warrior. Unaware of his proximity, the Seneca made camp and fell into a dreamy sleep, at which point the Catawba warrior stole one of their tomahawks and quietly hacked to death the entire pursuing party—still completely naked, of course. Though he was done with his tomahawking, the Catawba warrior was not quite finished with revenge. He threw on some dead man's blood-soaked clothes, grabbed the nicest rifle he could find, and hiked all the way back to the site of his initial capture, where the seven other dead Seneca still lay. There, he scalped each of the corpses and triumphantly returned home to his loving family and presumably peaceful day job.

 THE MANual

A BRIEF HISTORY OF THE BAYONET

Of all the weapons consistently employed by the military, none are as storied, feared, and damned old as the bayonet. The bayonet's story starts way back in Europe during the 1600s. As primitive firearms began to replace trusty bows for the hunting of wild animals, hunters discovered a troubling problem—if you missed the wild boar with your highly inaccurate, slow-loading musket, you were suddenly stuck holding a five-foot piece of iron and wood with a pissed-off, tusked boar ten yards away from you. Enter the bayonet.

After missing the bear, the last thing Jebediah remembered was where he'd left his bayonet.

BLOOD, SWEAT, AND TYRANNY

By the 1700s, bayonets were in use by the majority of gun-toting armies around the world. But they were never very trustworthy. Armies originally adopted "plug" bayonets—so named because they fit into the barrel of the gun and plugged up the musket, preventing it from being fired again—an innovation about as short-lived as the travel fax machine. But soon the bayonet evolved into an effective and deadly secondary weapon. With armies still drawing battle lines at close range, an imminent bayonet charge became a psychologically fierce assault tactic.

By the dawn of trench warfare, however, everything had changed. Nobody wanted to be fighting in a four-foot wide trench with a two-foot bayonet attached to a five-foot rifle. It was a great way to get yourself killed. So, bayonets began to take the shape we know today—medium-sized, multipurpose combat knives that gave soldiers a last-ditch chance at self-preservation.

Today, the standard-issue M9 (Army) and OKC-3S (Marine Corps) bayonets are about as far removed as possible from the spike bayonet of the 1800s. These modern incarnations are compact, ultra lightweight, and versatile as hell—they're designed to be used for everything from piercing body armor and cutting sheet metal to clipping wire and even opening bottles.

> "Only the dead have seen the end of war."
> —Damn true words from the Spanish poet George Santayana

 The MANual

CUTTING YOUR WRITING CHOPS IN THE TRENCHES

J.R.R. Tolkien

John Ronald Reuel Tolkien, author of *The Lord of the Rings*, didn't experience the same success in war as he did in writing about it. For starters, he delayed enlisting to finish school, and this was before hippies made draft evasion fashionable. Then, when he finally made it to the front lines in France as a member of the British Army, he managed to develop debilitating cases of both trench fever, a disease carried by lice, and trench foot from the constantly soggy conditions. He ended the war early, emaciated and in and out of hospitals.

Ernest Hemingway

Just four weeks on the front in World War I made a man of young Ernest Hemingway. He joined the war as an ambulance driver in 1918 and was deployed to Italy. Within a month of arriving, he was seriously injured by an exploding mortar shell. It was here that Hemingway's education really began. During his six-month hospital stay, he ogled, flirted with, and eventually successfully wooed a sexy Red Cross nurse named Agnes von Kurowsky.

The next year, Hemingway headed home with plans to marry his beloved nurse, only to get jilted when his betrothed fell for an Italian general and broke off their engagement. The turbulent experience became the inspiration for his first bestseller, *A Farewell to Arms*, as well as his lifelong phobia of long-term commitments.

C.S. Lewis

The Chronicles of Narnia author had some very real experiences to draw upon for his classic children's fantasy series. During WWI, the Englishman was deployed to France and saw combat the very day he turned nineteen. After successfully surviving several bloody skirmishes in the trenches, catastrophe struck and Lewis was badly injured by friendly fire when a British shell misfired, killing two of his friends.

A NATION'S GREATEST HONOR

In 1861, the senator from Iowa, James Grimes, introduced a bill to the Senate to establish a medal of honor for gallantry in the Navy. President Lincoln was all for it. Within two months, bills for Medals of Honor in both the Navy and the Army were signed into federal law. The Medal of Honor stands as the nation's highest military achievement, handed out for incredible bravery to individuals who have gone above and beyond their call of duty. In just over 150 years, 3,465 Medals of Honor have been handed out.

1. Since the beginning of World War II, the majority of the Medal of Honor recipients have received the honor posthumously. During World War II, 57 percent of the 464 Medals of Honor awarded were done so posthumously. In Vietnam, that percentage jumped to 62 percent. Of eleven military personnel awarded the medal in the most recent conflicts in Afghanistan and Iraq, only four have been alive to receive it.

During his epic seventy-two-year reign, French King Louis XIV never lost an argument or a war, possibly in part because he inscribed the words Ultima Ratio Regum (The Final Argument of Kings) on every one of his country's cannons.

IMPORTANT SURVIVAL SKILL 1

How to Evade a Sniper in the Jungle

1. ZIG The minute you realize you are under fire, zig. Make an erratic lateral movement, removing yourself from the line of fire.

2. ZAG After your initial zig, it's time to zag. Snipers easily track steady linear movement, so before its too late, abruptly shift toward the opposite direction. Make sure your zigging and zagging don't fit any pattern.

3. FLIP The more random your movements, the better your chances of survival. As you zig and zag, be sure to vary your body position. The sniper will be targeting your head or your chest, so make sure these vital body parts are changing position. Stop, drop, roll, do cartwheels or flips. This is when all those parkour lessons you never took would have come in handy.

4. HIDE As with most attacks, your long-term survival depends on your ability to find adequate cover. In the forest, this means looking for the biggest, healthiest tree and flinging yourself behind its loving woody trunk. Move from tree to tree until you find more permanent shelter, preferably a cushy building with concrete walls.

 THE MANual

> "A prisoner of war is a man who tries to kill you
> and fails, and then asks you not to kill him."
> —British Prime Minister Winston Churchill

2. Theodore Roosevelt is the only American president to ever have been awarded the Medal of Honor. He received it posthumously (in 2001) for heroically leading his regiment of Rough Riders in the bloody assault of San Juan Ridge, Cuba, during the Spanish-American War.

3. Fully qualified children of Medal of Honor recipients are given entry to any military academy of their choice. No questions asked.

4. The Army, Air Force, and Navy each have their own version of the medal. Recipients from the Marines and Coast Guard both receive the Navy's medal.

5. Former Hawaii Senator Daniel K. Inouye received his medal in 2000, joining an astonishing twenty other Japanese American Medal of Honor recipients from his unit, the 442nd Regimental Combat Team. The 442nd, made up almost entirely of US citizens of Japanese descent, stands as the most decorated unit in American history.

6. Two sets of fathers and sons have been awarded the Medal of Honor: Lt. Arthur MacArthur (Civil War) and his son General Douglas MacArthur (WWII), and Theodore Roosevelt (Spanish-American War) and his son Theodore Roos-

BLOOD, SWEAT, AND TYRANNY

evelt Jr. (WWII). Like his father, Theodore Roosevelt Jr. did not survive to receive his medal.

7. During the Civil War, Medals of Honor were handed out like party favors. At the time, the medal was only a couple years old and proper guidelines had not been set for handing it out. In 1863 alone, 864 medals were handed out to soldiers just for reenlisting in the US Army (they were rescinded fifty-four years later).

8. The youngest recipient of the Medal of Honor was eleven-year-old Willie Johnston, a Civil War drummer boy who gallantly held on to his drum while the rest of his grown-ass unit dropped everything they were carrying and retreated.

9. Recipients of the Medal of Honor are extended invitations to every presidential inauguration and inaugural ball for the rest of their lives.

10. Only one member of the US Coast Guard has ever received the Medal of Honor. Signalman First Class Douglas Munro personally led five Higgins boats in the rescue of a battalion of Marines pinned down by Japanese fire at Point Cruz, Guadalcanal. Signalman Munro positioned his own boat directly in the line of fire so the Marines could be evacuated to the other crafts. His final words were, "Did they get off?"

"War is hell."

—*Full-time General (and part-time crazy) William Tecumseh Sherman*

The MANual

FIVE REASONS TO RESPECT THE SAMURAI

A group of samurai chillaxing on a Friday night (c. 1865).

1. Divine Wind

Just as the samurai were gaining prominence in feudal Japan, the Mongol Empire, led by Genghis Khan's grandson Kublai, was busy building the largest, most savage empire Asia has ever known. They'd recently laid waste to Korea and now had their sights set on China, so in 1266 Khan sent a few minions to Japan to demand they send military assistance and accept him as their patriarch or accept the brutal consequences.

The prideful Japanese refused, and the Mongols never forgot. After they'd captured China, the Mongols turned their attentions across the Sea of Japan. Not one for half-assing an attack, Kublai sent an immense fleet of highly trained soldiers to lay siege to the Japanese coast. During the monsoon season of 1274, about 25,000 men landed in Hakata Bay on the island of Kyushu.

The Mongol soldiers were equipped with everything from poisonous arrows and swords to fricking ceramic grenades. But the fearless samurai, as we now know, were not the type to roll over and play obsequious, so they met their enemy on the beach on horseback. The samurai did the best they could, but they were outnumbered, outmatched, and pretty much shit-out-of-luck.

Despite losing the battle, the samurai were relentless enough to deplete their enemy's supply of arrows, and before night fell the Mongols retreated to their ships to avoid attack. That night, as if by divine providence, a great storm came and by morning the Mongol fleet had lost about 200 ships and perhaps 13,000 men.

Kublai Kan't

The Mongol's massive defeat during the Battle of Koan had a larger historical significance: it ended the previously unchecked spread of the Mongol Empire. Who knows, if it hadn't been for a little divine wind, we might all be Khans now.

Seven years later, Kublai's army returned, this time with two massive fleets (one Chinese and one Korean) totaling as many as 4,500 ships and 140,000 men, the largest seaborne military invasion the world would see until D-Day during WWII. The samurai, however, had built walls on several beaches and were better prepared for large-scale warfare.

The samurai's preparations and vigorous counterattacks (collectively referred to as the Battle of Koan or the Second Battle of Hakata Bay) forestalled the Mongolian fleet just long enough to let the gods take over. In June of 1281, a great typhoon, or kamikaze (divine wind), swept across land and water; massive, swarming waves pelted the ill-suited Mongolian ships and torrents of windswept raindrops the size of boulders beat down from above, sending as many as 100,000 Chinese, Koreans, and Mongolians to their watery graves and saving Japan from their would-be-captors.

2. Don't Bring a Long Sword to a Samurai Sword Fight

The samurai warriors had a remarkable arsenal of weapons at their disposal: kama (dual-purpose farming sickles), tessen (fake folding paper fans made of solid steel), daikyu (power-

> "One who is samurai must before all things, keep constantly in mind, by day and by night ... that he has to die."
> —Daidoji Yuzan

ful longbows), and kabuto wari (helmet-splitting clubs). But no weapon is as well known and respected as the katana, the samurai sword.

Delicate Mayhem

For such a formidable weapon, the katana is notoriously finicky. The swords must be stored blade up, or they quickly lose their edge. They also require constant maintenance—they must be kept well oiled to prevent the blade from rusting.

During the Middle Ages, when Europeans were bludgeoning each other to death with brittle long swords, the samurai had perfected the art of bladesmithing by folding together both high- and low-carbon steels to allow for both elastic durability and razor sharpness. Beside the gut-piercing tip, the blade of the katana was slightly curved, greatly increasing the efficacy of each strike by reducing the contact area. This meant that each blow with a katana was a blow with a perfect edge so sharp and powerful it could literally slice an English long sword in half.

But, just in case the katana wasn't ass-kicking enough, the samurai also carried a smaller version, the ritualistic wakizashi sword, that was used solely to allow the warrior to easily commit ritualistic suicide, presumably for embarrassing his finely crafted katana.

3. The Honorable Exit

The samurai had rituals for everything from preparing for battle to pouring tea, so there's really nothing weird about the fact that life's big events, like dying, were done strictly by the book. For the samurai, seppuku, which means "self disembowelment," was the preferred method for exiting the planet.

The technique went something like this: if a samurai was shamed in battle, dishonored his master, or was facing imminent capture, he would draw his short sword, plunge it into the left side of his abdomen, and draw it quickly across his stomach and then upward. For those intent on showing true courage, they would follow this gut-spilling cut with a second violent incision from the top of the abdomen downward.

This method of suicide was neither painless nor at all quick and the samurai normally bled to death slowly.

Eventually, the powers-that-were in Japan started using seppuku as the preferred method of execution as well. In order to allow a condemned prisoner the honor of taking his own life, the man was asked to kneel on a tatami mat where he was presented a small table with a short sword and given the opportunity to perform his own execution. Immediately upon

A Not-So-Instantaneous Exit

After being severed from the body, the human head remains conscious for up to eight seconds.

committing the act, a friend or relative of the condemned would raise a katana and decapitate the dying prisoner, thus ending the suffering but keeping his honor intact.

Ritualistic seppuku ceremony in Kobe, Japan (1868).

4. The Way of the Warrior

During the Second World War, the insular island nation of Japan, a fledgling world power with just 100 million people, was able to wage war on an overwhelmingly stronger United States (as well as Britain, Australia, Canada, the Republic of China, and Russia simultaneously) for more than 1,000 blood-soaked days. How did the Japanese accomplish such a tremendous feat? One word: Bushido.

Literally translated as "The Way of the Warrior," the Bushido code evolved slowly—over nearly a millennium of feudal warfare—from a combination of Confucianism, Zen Buddhism, Shintoism, and the militaristic teachings of Japan's noble warrior class, the samurai. Bushido was composed of very simple, yet powerful tenets: loyalty, courage, mastering the crap out of martial arts, self-control, mercy (albeit limited), and, above all, honor to your family, ruler, and country until death.

The code originally rose to prominence starting in the 1400s when Japan was a very fractured set of islands. Shoguns and warlords rose and fell faster than stalks of rice and the samurai had to abide by the strict set of morals just to keep total anarchy from sweeping over the land. Over the centuries to come, the rules of conduct solidified and, during the long, stable Tokugawa Shogunate (1603–1868), the Bushido code went from an unspoken set of ideals to the actual law of the land.

By the time Pearl Harbor rolled around, Japan's entire military had been steeped in the Bushido code. For the Japanese, the mindset helped create a hardened force to be reckoned with in the Pacific, but also led to tragic consequences—from banzai suicide charges and kamikaze air raids to the abhorrent treatment of enemy prisoners of war and foreign civilians.

5. Miyamoto Musashi

In samurai culture, the term rōnin was designated for wandering samurai warriors who had become masterless. Some arrived at this bastard state upon the death of their master;

others had simply been disowned. Miyamoto Musashi, on the other hand, seems to have simply inherited the position from the gods themselves. Why? Because Miyamoto Musashi may have been the greatest sword fighter in history.

Musashi's early life is as mysterious as it damn ought to be. He might as well have been forged from the discarded steel at the Kyoto Katanaworks or crawled out of a dragon's recently disemboweled intestines, because the fury he brought to Japan was magical. Rumor had it that he was born in the Harima Province on the island of Honshu, the son of a famous swordsman named Shinmen Munisai, who had placed a katana in the hands of young Miyamoto while he was still nursing.

Regardless of his early years, Musashi burst onto the samurai scene out of nowhere right around the time his body slipped stealthily into puberty. At the age of thirteen, Musashi answered a written call for dueling partners posted by a (fully grown) traveling samurai by the name of Arima Kihei. Kihei, apparently unfazed with having to fight a mere child, attacked Musashi with a short sword only to have the thirteen-year-old Musashi beat him to death with a wooden staff.

After his first duel, Musashi hung around home for a couple years waiting for his voice to drop. Then he hit the road to tour the countryside in what is called a *musha shogyu*, basically the most terrifying coming-of-age imaginable where young samurais wander the countryside looking to hone their skills.

As coming-of-age stories are wont to do, Musashi's took a weird and unexpected turn when he somehow found himself fighting as a paid warrior in some ill-fated battles. Whatever happened during this time, it's around then that he decides to focus on fighting duels with only a wooden sword.

A couple years later, around the time he was legally allowed to drink sake, Musashi wandered into the renowned Yoshioka Martial Arts School and challenged the school's master and namesake, Yoshioka Seijuro, to a duel. Seijuro happily accepted, only to become enraged when Musashi showed up to the duel super late and carrying nothing but his wooden replica of a sword. When Seijuro attacked him, Musashi brutally smacked him in the arm with his fake sword, crippling the master martial artist for life.

When Seijuro's brother challenged Musashi for revenge, Musashi dispatched him in the same brutal manner. Taking out the two star martial arts masters of one of the best martial arts schools in Japan did not go over well with the people around town and, before he knew it, Musashi was facing off against a whole clan of swordsmen. At this point, Musashi realized he was in a bind and gave up the fake sword, drawing both his katana *and* ritualistic wakizashi short sword (which nobody ever fought with) and went about slicing and dicing his way through the whole crowd, inventing his own brand new duel-sword fighting style along the way.

Once he'd killed the head of the clan, he moseyed on out of town and up to Hozoin where he had heard there were

BLOOD, SWEAT, AND TYRANNY

IMPORTANT SURVIVAL SKILL 2

FIVE EASY STEPS TO SURVIVING A HAND GRENADE ATTACK

1. DIVE Don't run. If the grenade explodes while you're running, surprise, you'll get a back full of shrapnel. Instead, hit the floor face first and with your head as far away from the grenade as possible.

2. FEET TOWARD THE GRENADE Position the soles of your feet toward the grenade and, for your children's sake, close your damn legs. This way, the soles of your shoes (and feet) will absorb most of the oncoming shrapnel.

3. COVER Pull your elbows into your ribs to protect your vital organs and cover your ears and head. It's about to get loud.

4. CLOSE YOUR EYES AND SAY AHHHHH There's going to be a shock-blast, so close your eyes and open your mouth to keep your lungs from exploding.

some monks he could fight who were masters of the lance. Mushashi kept this lifestyle up for another couple years, alternating between fighting duels, meditating, and working in the fields with the Japanese peasants. During one duel, Musashi's opponent, a master martial artist named Muso, was so inspired by Musashi's fighting style he crafted a new school of staff fighting around the experience.

Finally, at the ripe old age of 30, Musashi packed up his dueling trophies and retired. He spent the remaining thirty-one years of his life perfecting his two-handed sword fighting technique and teaching students who were just glad they didn't really have to fight him.

Gatling's Good Intentions

In the 1860s, Dr. Richard Gatling set about inventing a rapid-fire, "automatic" gun. The purpose? To reduce the future casualties of war. How would more bullets flying at the same time help reduce war dead? Well, at the time, wars were fought by lining up entire armies within shouting distance of one another and yelling "fire," so Gatling believed that if you could replace all those rifle-wielding foot soldiers with one guy cranking out rounds, a lot less souls would be lost. It was a great thought, but the tactics of warfare were not about to keep up with his newfangled technology; the sizes of armies grew and the result was the bloodiest century in world history—thanks in part to Gatling's highly effective invention.

FIVE BLOODY POWERS

Cracker Jacks, Here, Get Your Cracker Jacks

The violent 500-year reign of the Roman Empire can be summed up in one monumental edifice: the Colosseum.

> ### The House that Vespasian Built
> The Colosseum could seat just over 50,000 spectators, about the same as Yankee Stadium. But the Yankees still suck.

Where today we watch men in tight pants chase little balls in places like Petco Park and Tropicana Field, citizens of Rome filed into the Amphitheatrum Flavium to watch blood sports, including detailed battle reenactments, exotic animal hunts, and gladiator-on-gladiator death matches.

Gladiators fought one another with spears, swords, and bows. Sometimes, during halftime, patrons could watch men pitted against wild rhinos, hippos, elephants, lions, tigers, panthers, and crocodiles.

Nine thousand animals were slaughtered during its inaugural games alone and, by the time Rome collapsed, nearly half a million people had fought and died on arena's hallowed floor.

 THE MANual

Bred into Empire

By the time it reached its peak, the Mongol Empire covered 16 percent of the earth's surface. It was the largest contiguous empire in history. But its most lasting legacy isn't on the ground; it may be in your blood.

When Genghis Khan was just a young man, a rival tribe kidnapped his wife and something inside of him snapped. He unified several Mongol-Turkic tribes, annihilated his enemy, and rescued his wife. But he didn't stop. He proceeded to sweep across the Eurasian continent, swallowing village after village.

It turns out Genghis Khan wasn't just a fighter; he was a lover, and apparently a prolific one at that. As he sacked villages throughout Asia, he would have every man and pregnant woman killed before bringing in the surviving fertile women to spread his seed. Genghis Khan had a lot of seed. Though his empire no longer exists, his legacy lives on in today's world population—as many as one out of every 200 people alive today are blood relations to Genghis Khan.

"In peace, sons bury their fathers. In war, fathers bury their sons."
—*Greek philosopher Herodotus*

The Empire on Which the Sun Never Sets

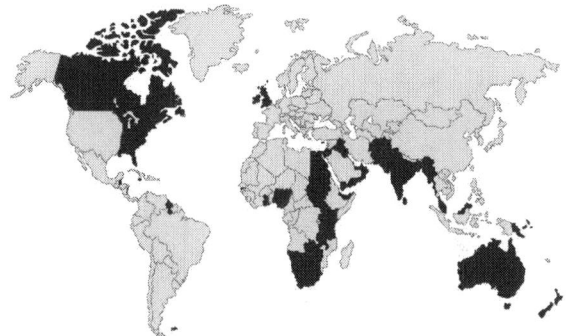

Portion of the world previously forced to play cricket (British Empire).

Why are the proper, crumpet-sampling Brits on a list of the bloodiest powers in history? Because they were most likely the bloodiest. During more than 400 years of global rule, the British Empire engaged in over 100 individual wars, killing as many as 100,000,000 of the planet's inhabitants through violence, disease, and famine.

Before its rapid decline after WWII, the British Empire had earned the nickname "the Empire on which the sun never sets," so large that the sun was always shining on it somewhere.

Back to the Farm

Sometimes violent takeovers aren't ignited abroad; they burn from within. That's what happened in the 1970s in Cambodia

THE MANUAL

when, at the height of Communism's sweep over Southeast Asia, the Communist Party of Kamphuchea grabbed power.

THE NEW GREAT EMPIRE?

At its height, the British Empire, the most expansive in history, commanded over 20 percent of the planet's population. Today, the People's Republic of China rules over 1.35 billion people, or 19 percent of the world's population.

Little was strange about the rise of the Communist Party in a country next door to Vietnam and China, but what happened in Cambodia is one of the most bizarre and disturbing episodes in modern history. The Khmer Rouge, as the Communist Party became known, were obsessed with farming. The party dreamt of a completely self-sufficient agrarian society for the Cambodia of tomorrow. So they went about building it.

The Khmer Rouge forcibly moved everyone living in Cambodia's cities to the countryside. Citizens with no farming experience in their entire lives were forced to adapt to their new situation or starve. Those who disobeyed were simply killed. By the end of their short, drastic social experiment, the Khmer Rouge had managed to murder nearly two million of their own citizens; another estimated two million Cambodians died from starvation and disease. In the end, the population of Cambodia was cut in half.

Shrinky Dink

You may have never heard of the Shuar people, a seminomadic, semi-terrifying Amazonian tribe from modern-day Ecuador and Peru, but you're surely familiar with their work: shrunken heads.

The Shuar, who were constantly feuding with neighboring factions, are a spiritual people who believed that a dead enemy was still a dangerous enemy. Thus, a successful skirmish was measured not by a count of bodies left on the battlefield, but by the number of shrunken enemy's heads, called *tsantsa*, in the victorious Shuar's trophy case. (The purpose of the shrinking was superstition—they believed shrinking the head would trap the person's soul and prevent it from seeking revenge.)

But the Shuar aren't just famous for their head collection. Fiercely prideful of their homeland and their freedom, the Shuar repeatedly beat back every invading people who approached—first fending off the Inca and then the Spanish. Who knows, maybe some superstitions work. They remain an independent tribe to this day.

REVENGE IS A DISH BEST SERVED GOLD

When the Spanish came in to the Shuar lands looking for riches, the Shuar fought back and captured the governor of the Spanish-held Logrono region. They gave him one of the most symbolically apt executions ever—pouring scalding-hot molten gold down the man's throat.

 THE MANual

W IS FOR WAR...ELEPHANT

Elephants are one of earth's most intelligent, trainable, and deadly animals. They weigh in at about five tons, have inch-thick skin, and can move at almost 20 miles per hour. They are essentially living, breathing, crapping tanks. And man has known it for centuries. Unlike a horse, which will neigh and whinny and carefully step over an enemy body in battle, elephants just go ahead and trample them to death, which made them history's fiercest cavalry.

Death by Dumbo

If you thought death by electric chair was inhumane, imagine living in a world where a condemned criminal was executed by an elephant stepping on their head. As recently as the nineteenth century, rulers living in India and Southeast Asia used highly trained Asian elephants to do just that—one of the most horrific methods of capital punishment ever invented.

Morte Elephantum

Execution by elephant made it all the way to the Roman Empire, where the preferred method of execution was decapitation, or *capitalis*. From the Latin word caput, meaning "head," it is the root of our modern term, "capital punishment."

But head crushing was just the beginning, and the powerful royals who administered these barbaric punishments were always eager to employ a new method of elephant-induced agony. They had their pachyderm executioners taught to use their trunks to toy with prisoners before ripping their limbs from their bodies. They even attached sword-like contraptions to their tusks to allow the elephants to slash up the condemned.

The Alps Are but Snowy Hills

> *"I swear so soon as age will permit…I will use fire and steel to arrest the destiny of Rome."*
> —*A pimple-faced teenage Hannibal to his father Hamilcar Barca*

Choosing to go to war against Rome in the 200s BC is like you offering to jump into the ring with Mike Tyson circa 1985. But that's exactly what Hannibal Barca did when he led a Carthaginian Army over the Italian Alps and directly into the heart of the Roman Republic. While most Mediterranean powers were happy just to maintain a scrap of autonomy, Hannibal wanted an empire.

Hannibal's illustrious career as one of history's greatest military minds began around 221 BC when he took control of his father's army in modern-day Spain. After consolidating his power on the Iberian Peninsula, Hannibal was popular, cocky, and immensely powerful. And when Rome tried to crash his party by allying themselves with the city of Saguntum (south of Barcelona), Hannibal sacked it and started a war with the most powerful empire on earth.

Not to half-ass his first real war, in 218 Hannibal began one of the most epic and fabled journeys in military history: crossing the Italian Alps with nearly 38,000 foot soldiers, 8,000 horsemen, and, brazenly, thirty-seven war elephants.

The war elephants, probably a now-extinct subspecies of the African elephant known as Atlas elephants, were ill-suited to make the arduous journey across the snow-plastered Alps. Not only did they require a lot of food, but their large size made narrow passages across the icy cliffs a nightmare. Some elephants starved to death; others fell to their deaths. Still, at least one elephant survived the journey: the one Hannibal most often rode.

Despite the loss of most of their elephantry and perhaps as much as half the infantry, Hannibal's arrival from the Alps took Rome by total surprise. He swiftly won two battles in Trebia and Lake Trasimene, liberating tribes that quickly allied with him. Thus the war raged on, with Hannibal outsmarting the Romans at every turn. Hannibal was so successful, in fact, that he spent the next fifteen years tearing up the Italian Peninsula. By the end of his campaign, Hannibal had amassed an army large enough to sack Rome. But Carthage's government stalled on the decision.

Then around 212 BC, the Romans realized the best tactic against Hannibal was simply to ignore him completely. They turned their attentions across the Mediterranean Sea and attacked Carthage's Sicilian territories, and Hannibal's threat to Rome began to weaken. Though he held on in the Italian Peninsula for another decade, his victories were diminishing. Eventually, with the Roman armies approaching their homeland, Carthage recalled Hannibal to Africa, ending the campaign completely and ushering in an unsteady peace.

For a time, Hannibal tried politics on for size, and in 200 BC he became the chief magistrate of Carthage, restoring some of the kingdom's luster. Hannibal's renewed power frightened Rome and they demanded his surrender. Instead, he went into exile, voluntarily of course, and for a time lived a life on the road. When the Romans finally tracked him down and ordered his execution, he still disobeyed, choosing instead to take some poison and leave behind a letter that, roughly translated, read: "Let us relieve the Romans from the anxiety they have so long experienced, since they think it tries their patience too much to wait for an old man's death."

Not Your Average Joust

> *"My brother, why do you hide yourself in the canopy shadows? Let us fight the elephant battle for our own honors. No future kings will do what we are going to do."*
> —Siamese King Naresuan to Minchit Sra, the Crown Prince of Burma

Truer words have rarely been spoken: no two monarchs would ever fight to the death atop elephants again. Which is unfortunate because elephant-mounted death matches are pretty much the tits when it comes to working out differences.

> The Kingdom of Siam employed war elephants as late as the Franco-Siamese War at the end of the nineteenth century.

At the height of the Burma-Siam war in 1591, King Naresuan challenged the crown prince of Burma to a joust to the death atop war elephants. The battle ended quickly, when Naresuan managed to deliver a decisive deathblow to Sra with his lance. The Elephant Battle victory essentially ended the war, and today is still celebrated in Thailand.

THREE TECHNOLOGICAL INNOVATIONS THAT CAME OUT OF BEING SUPER PARANOID ABOUT THE SOVIETS

The Interwebs

During the 1960s, the skittish US government commissioned several agencies to research ways to remotely connect sensitive data networks in different corners of the country into nationally connected super networks. The goal was to provide an information system broad enough to survive the localized nuclear attacks they believed were imminent.

By the early 1990s, the now-global networks were opened to the public for commercial use and became known colloquially as the Internet, the World Wide Web, the web, and someday simply as the AWWWWW, Cats!

GPS

In 1960, the world's first Global Positioning System, named "Transit," could give an accurate location anywhere in the world once every sixty minutes using five satellites to triangulate the position. Its purpose was to stop nuclear attacks from the USSR by developing a real-time method for tracking

THE MANual

bombers, subs, and even Intercontinental Ballistic Missiles (ICBMs). Although, in a world where ICBMs traveled at 13,000 mph, it's hard to see how a once-an-hour GPS system was quite up to snuff (since Washington D.C. and Moscow are only 4,800 miles apart).

No, you are not using traditional GPS to precisely guide your way to the bar with your iPhone. But you are using something similar. During WWII, the military used the LORAN system that fixed ship position using ground-based radio receivers, a system very similar to today's cell triangulation using cell towers and Wi-Fi hotspots. But don't fret, you are still more tech savvy than your grandparents: current smartphones are also assisted by satellite-based GPS to help get that extra-precise distance between you and your next pint.

Digital Photography

Before digital photography, spy satellites still relied on good old-fashioned film to take top secret recon photos. The only problem was that the image was stuck in the film canister, the film canister was stuck in satellite, and the satellite was stuck in space. So every top secret roll of film had to be ejected through the atmosphere and allowed to float down to earth with a tiny parachute. During one disastrous spy mission, a broken parachute lead to a canister plummeting 16,000 feet into the Pacific Ocean. It took the Navy three deep-sea search missions to find it.

Things finally improved in the 1960s with the Kennan-11, a digital imaging system that could relay real-time photos to the Navy.

Today digital photography has all but replaced its tangible predecessor and allowed for the myriad drinking photos posted on social media that help us document this important era in post–Cold War history.

Seven World War II Military Innovations You See Every Day

The Jumbo jet

Today's Boeing and Airbus fleets owe their beginnings to Nazi Germany's revolutionary Messerschmitt Me 262, the world's first operational jet fighter. Although there were never enough produced to swing the tide of World War II, the Messerschmitt terrifyingly outperformed all Allied fighters at the time and helped usher in the age of the jet engine.

Walkie-talkies

A Canadian invention, the walkie-talkie, known more boringly as "the handheld receiver," was originally used for two-way communication between military personnel during the war.

Random Terrifying Fact: At least fifty active nuclear weapons, most of them Russian, are currently designated "lost at sea."

Today most militaries use far superior communication technologies, but walkie-talkies are still extremely popular among both children and rent-a-cops.

Duct tape

During WWII, the US military joined forces with Johnson & Johnson to create an adhesive tape that could be torn by hand and used to create a waterproof seal for ammunition cases.

Called duck tape by soldiers, the impressive tape was so effective that soldiers were soon using it for MacGyver-esque stopgap repairs on everything from dungarees to guns and Jeeps to fighter planes.

The microwave oven

The microwave oven actually has its origins in a completely different technology: radar. Britain's Royal Air Force was first in successfully tracking enemy aircrafts approaching British shores using radio waves, technology they termed "Chain Home" and that later became known as RADAR (Radio Detection and Ranging).

As the technology advanced, scientists discovered the microwave, a wavelength that resonates at the same frequency as water molecules, thus producing heat and revolutionizing leftovers.

Silly Putty

The happiest accident of the war was undoubtedly the invention of Silly Putty, a bizarre substance discovered by scientists

BLOOD, SWEAT, AND TYRANNY

IMPORTANT SURVIVAL SKILL 3
How to Survive a Nuclear Attack

1. FIND SHELTER Caves are a good choice, as are deep rivulets and crevasses in the terrain. If you have none, dig as fast as possible. As a last result, go indoors and hope for the best.

2. LOOK AWAY FROM THE BLAST An atomic bomb explodes with the same brightness as the sun and this is not the time to go blind.

3. AVOID THE FALLOUT No, the black water falling from the sky is not potable. After the explosion, scalding hot chunks of radiated dust clouds known as black rain will plummet back down to earth. This black rain is almost as deadly as the initial blast.

4. STAY INDOORS Stay in your shelter for at least eight days to allow the atmospheric radiation to clear.

5. FIND SUSTENANCE Water: Groundwater is contaminated—do not drink it. Instead, seek well water. Always boil and filter. Building water is also safe: In the likely event that the water isn't running, you may extract the water trapped in piping.

Food: Puncture-free cans of food are good to go. Animals are edible, however, remember to skin the carcass and toss the heart, liver, and kidneys, which have by now absorbed deadly levels of radioactive toxins. Avoid meat close to the now radioactive bones. Eschew aboveground fruits and vegetables in favor of root vegetables like potatoes and carrots.

6. FORAGE IN THICK CLOTHING Wear goggles, gloves, hats, and long-sleeved shirts or jackets. You don't need to worry about looking cool; there's nobody left.

struggling to invent a replacement silicone-based synthetic rubber. Grown children all over the world can thank Japan for occupying most of the world's rubber-producing regions, forcing America to think outside the egg.

The Jeep

Suburban soccer moms and gas-guzzling off-road enthusiasts everywhere are forever indebted to the United States Army, who commissioned Ford and Wyllis-Overland to build the world's most famous sport utility vehicle, the GPW, which was quickly nicknamed the Jeep. There were about 640,000 Jeeps in operation during the war, including one failed amphibious model that royally sucked on both land and water.

Hot pink fishnets

Nylon was originally invented in 1940 as a cheap replacement for the costly silk and hemp used in parachute chords. Today it lives the glamorous life, making up everything from guitar strings and pantyhose to car engine parts and tires.

"Certainly there is no hunting like the hunting of man and those who have hunted armed men long enough and liked it, never really care for anything else thereafter."

—*Ernest Hemingway*

Meat

History in the Flesh

In 1976, America had a great year. We celebrated the bicentennial of the Declaration of Independence. We landed spacecraft on Mars. *Rocky* roared into movie theatres from Los Angeles to Philadelphia. The VCR was invented. But what eclipsed all of those unparalleled causes for celebration was that 1976 was the beefiest year in our country's glorious history. During that year, Americans consumed an average of 89 pounds of beef *per person*. That's a quarter-pounder every day.

Since then, it's hard to say that meat hasn't lost a little bit of its *je ne sais quoi*. More people are eating veggie burgers. Even the manliest of men are concerned about terms like "cholesterol," "heart disease," and "death." But the glory of meat will live on as it has lived for 50,000 years. Meat has helped craft our history, our biology, and our cultures. It will live on in our hearts (literally) and in our colons (very literally. Seriously, it takes forever to clean it out of your colon. John Wayne was full of meat when he died). Sorry, we digress. We dedicate this section to the glory that is edible flesh.

MEAT

THE ORIGINAL ERA OF BIG-GAME HUNTING

When you think of big-game hunting, the first thing that comes to mind is the bygone era of the early 1900s, when "going on safari" meant shooting animals, not photographing them. But the truth is that the real era of big-game hunting wasn't in this century. Or this millennium. The biggest and most impressive hunting feats happened way back about 13,000 years ago. And the animals our human ancestors hunted, and eventually killed off, were so much more massive, dangerous, and exotic than what we know today, we can only begin to imagine what it was like.

By the time the Europeans arrived in the New World, the landscape looked a lot different than it had when the continent's first human inhabitants arrived. While bears, buffalo, and mountain lions still roamed the vast wilderness, many spectacular species of megafauna had long since been wiped out by skilled hunters and the changing climate.

American mastodon: Believe it or not, North America once had thriving elephant populations of its own—the elephant's relative, the forest-dwelling mastodon. Spread across the country from Alaska to the Rio Grande and from California to Florida, the American mastodon was a formidable presence. Bull mastodons grew to over nine feet tall, weighing in at four tons.

Mammoth: Almost everyone knows the woolly species of this now-extinct genus. But at one point, mammoths roamed Europe, Asia, North America, and Central America, with species as different from one another as a wolf is from a shih tzu. In Siberia, the massive steppe mammoth stood 15 feet tall, the same height as a one-story house. But it was the woolly mammoth of Europe and North America that played a vital role in human hunting and survival for almost 30,000 years. In the cave paintings found throughout Europe, woolly mammoths were among the most popular animals. Early man had an almost spiritual relationship with the woolly mammoth; they built their homes from mammoth bones, buried their dead alongside mammoth tusks, and, in some brutally cold winters, eked out survival only thanks to the mammoth's meat. When the Bering Land Bridge opened between Asia and North America, early man followed the mammoth migration from Alaska to Kansas.

In case you were wondering, the Biggest Bear in the Woods title now belongs to the polar bear. Males can weigh as much as 1,500 pounds.

Ground sloth: While the modern sloth has a reputation as a benign, lazy species, the giant ground sloth of yore was anything but. Growing as long as 20 feet from head to tail and with massive, powerful frames, the now-extinct ground sloths hold a place among the largest land animals of all time. Thanks to their thick, protective hides, massive size, and long, sharp claws, the ground sloths were a difficult prey to take down. Early human hunters in both North and South America had to get precariously close to the sloths to kill them, making the animals one of the most dangerous big game.

Smilodon (saber-toothed tiger): Although not technically tigers, the Smilodon certainly earned the "saber-toothed" portion of its well-known nickname. With giant, spear-like canines that could grow to nearly a foot long, powerful, compact, 800-pound bodies, and strong forearms, the Smilodon was an adept killer. Surprisingly, the Smilodon's jaw was significantly weaker compared to that of other carnivorous cats, so researchers postulate that instead of trying to quickly snap their prey's windpipe, the Smilodon would use its giant, knife-like teeth to pierce its pinned prey's jugular, resulting in a swift death from blood loss. The Smilodon lived throughout North and South America until as recently as 8000 BC, when the changing climate and competition from human hunters dwindled its population.

American lion: It may sound even more out there than a forest-dwelling North American elephant, but this continent was once patrolled by giant, fierce lions. What's perhaps even more frightening is that these cats were about 25 percent larger than today's African lions, possibly making them the largest felines ever. A fully grown male lion stood about eight feet long and weighed over 900 pounds. Using keen intelligence, brute strength, and group hunting skills, these extremely savvy predators fed on pretty much any meaty thing they could sink their teeth into, including deer, bison, camels, and even mammoths. Making matters worse for the first humans to arrive in North America, these lions were fairly awesome at hide-and-seek when they cozied up in grass-lined caves during cold winters.

Short-faced bear: An abundant genus of bear hunted voraciously throughout western North America up until about 11,000 years ago, subsisting on about 35 pounds of fresh flesh every single day. Weighing in at over 2,000 pounds and able to stand to 15 feet, the short-faced bear was the largest bear in history. In fact, they may have been the largest land-roaming, carnivorous mammal ever.

IT'S A BIRD-EAT-BIRD WORLD: HAAST'S EAGLE

Not only did New Zealand have the largest flightless bird, it also had the world's largest eagle. Though their ten-foot wingspans were rather stubby for their 25-pound bodies, the Haast's Eagle's were incredible hunters, swooping down on their favorite food, the flightless moa, at speeds exceeding 50 miles per hour. Europeans visiting the islands for the first time were told tales of the eagles carrying off people as well.

Australia and New Zealand

When humans first migrated Down Under, perhaps as far back as 60,000 years ago, they found a continent of freaks. Actually it was a bit of a nightmare. Aside from your run-of-the-mill venomous snakes, spiders, and scorpions, there were also giant venomous lizards, man-snatching birds, and freakish flightless birds.

Megalania: Possibly the most terrifying animal ever, the megalania was as close to Godzilla as nature has ever come. Growing to an estimated size of 25 feet and perhaps as large as 4,000 pounds, the megalania was a supersized version of the equally vicious Komodo dragon. Being the largest lizard ever to crawl out of the ocean was apparently not enough for the megalania; it also carried a lethal cocktail of venom and infectious bacteria.

Giant moa: If you have a phobia of *Sesame Street*'s Big Bird, stop reading now. Because the giant moa put that big yellow chicken to shame. Growing to a freakish 12 feet tall and weighing perhaps as much as 600 pounds, moas were the largest bird-like things since the dinosaurs. Unfortunately for their existence, the moa couldn't fly, which made them particularly easy prey for the Polynesians who settled New Zealand. The Maori finally prepared their last giant moa meal sometime around the start of the fifteenth century.

The MANual

A TASTING GUIDE TO EXOTIC ANIMALS

Of course, you don't have to go back in time to sink your teeth into some strange creatures. Here's a brief tasting guide to today's more exotic dishes.

Crocodile
- *Found in:* Egypt, Kenya, Tanzania
- *Tastes like:* fishy turkey
- *Typical dishes:* tail fillets are pan-fried, deep-fried, or barbecued

Alligator
- *Found in:* Australia, Thailand, South Africa, Cuba
- *Tastes like:* crabby chicken
- *Typical dishes:* tail fillets are fried, barbecued, or used in soup

Turtle
- *Found in:* Cayman Islands, southern United States, China, Korea
- *Tastes like:* gamey veal
- *Typical dish:* soup

MEAT

Bison
- *Found in:* North America
- *Tastes like:* lean, flavorful beef
- *Typical dishes:* steaks, roasts, or burgers

Cockroach
- *Found in:* Thailand
- *Tastes like:* flavorless (absorbs the flavor of the oil in which it's prepared)
- *Typical dishes:* boiled or deep-fried

Grasshopper
- *Found in:* Mexico, China, Uganda
- *Tastes like:* light, crunchy, and earthy
- *Typical dish:* fried with salt and lime

Camel
- *Found in:* Saudi Arabia, Kenya, Libya, Kazakhstan
- *Tastes like:* very coarse, loose beef; very tough
- *Typical dish:* lightly fried with salt and pepper

Ox Testicle
- *Found in:* western United States, western Canada
- *Tastes like:* chewy liver
- *Typical dish:* deep-fried with a tasty dippin' sauce

Yak
- *Found in:* Himalayan regions of Tibet and Nepal, Mongolia, Russia
- *Tastes like:* rich, very lean red meat
- *Typical dishes:* steak, fillet, or ground into patties

Caribou (reindeer)
- *Found in:* Canada, Alaska, Sweden, Russia
- *Tastes like:* chewy lamb/beef hybrid with a strong livery aftertaste
- *Typical dishes:* steak, casserole

Zebra
- *Found in:* Namibia
- *Tastes like:* sweet, lean, juicy beef
- *Typical dish:* steak (medium rare recommended)

Guinea pig
- *Found in:* Peru, Bolivia, the Democratic Republic of Congo
- *Tastes like:* rabbit with a crispy, delicious skin
- *Typical dish:* slow-roasted whole

Kangaroo
- *Found in:* Australia
- *Tastes like:* tender, wild, and intense meat flavor
- *Typical dish:* steak or ground into patties

Diet Down Under: Kangatarianism

One of the hottest lifestyle diets in Australia is kangatarianism, the forgoing of all other meats except for the occasional kangaroo steak. Australians claim that eating wild kangaroo is much more ethical than eating farm-raised animals, kangaroos aren't harmful to the environment, and they aren't butchered in inhumane slaughterhouses.

Nutria (river rat)
- *Found in:* southern United States
- *Tastes like:* light chicken
- *Typical dish:* gumbo

Rattlesnake
- *Found in:* United States, Nicaragua, Peru
- *Tastes like:* mix between chicken, frog, and turtle
- *Typical dish:* fried in bite-sized pieces

 THE MANual

HOW TO KILL AND COOK A POISONOUS SNAKE

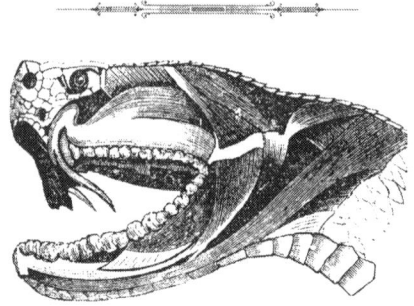

There are over 3,000 species of snake on the planet and fewer than 400 of them are poisonous. Snakes are naturally shy animals, so don't go out killing them for sport. But if you end up winning a mano-y-serpiente battle with a venomous serpent, you might as well not let it go to waste. Here are the five steps to cooking a snake.

Cut Off the Head

Most snakes' sack-like venom glands lie above the mouth behind the eyes, so make sure to cut an ample amount of distance down the body to ensure the elimination of any toxins. In addition, you'll need to make sure the snake hasn't recently poisoned and consumed any other animal. A poisoned and consumed rodent will retain its toxicity until fully digested by the snake.

Strip the Skin

Next you'll need to cut the skin off the same way you would a fish. Depending on the size of the snake, the thick skin should tear off the body fluidly.

Remove the Guts

Make a long incision along the snake's belly. This will open up the abdominal cavity, allowing you to pull out the guts.

Rinse and Soak the Meat

Snake meat looks like a cross between chicken and fish. But it tastes little like either. Snake meat is naturally tough, gamey, and a bit messy. Rinse the meat thoroughly, fillet the snake into four-inch chunks at the same angle as the ribs, and, if you have the time, allow it to soak in salt water for a full day to remove the gamey taste and texture.

Bread and Fry

Unlike a nice steak, snake meat needs a bit of help in the taste department. Bread the fillets with egg, flour, black pepper, and salt. Heat up either vegetable or canola oil and fry the snake fillets until golden brown.

The antivenin for the African black mamba's deadly bite is created by injecting the snake's diluted toxin into a sheep and then harvesting the antibodies for human use?

BEEF

Origin of the Steak: The Aurochs

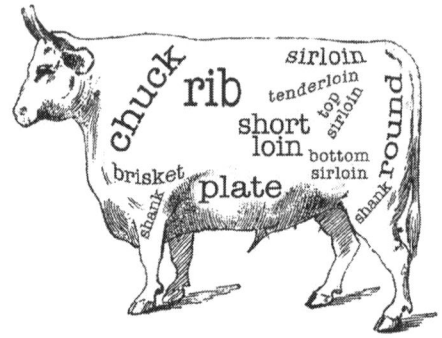

Imagine an angry bull charging you at full speed. Now imagine that same bull faster, angrier, more athletic, and with larger horns. Now you've got a good picture of the wild cows our ancestors had to deal with.

More than two million years ago, the world's climate became seasonal, cool, and dry, very similar to our world today, and vast expanses of grassland opened up throughout Europe and the Indian subcontinent. The explosion of grassland opened a new world to large grazing animals like the antelope, bison, and one particular animal whose descendants would one day inhabit every continent on the planet: the aurochs.

> Contrary to popular belief, bulls are not enraged by the color red.
> In fact, they can't even see it; they're red-green colorblind.

The aurochs had a lot more in common with a bull bred to fight in the Spanish bullring than with the modern cow. They were calm, fairly docile herders, but only until they were provoked. And provocation didn't require a spear in the back; these animals hated just being teased, striking their tormentors with three-foot horns before chucking them effortlessly with 1,500 pounds of muscle.

But despite a mercurial temperament, there were few animals on the grasslands as easy to get close to. And around 10,000 years ago, the early settlers of Mesopotamia roped them up and began to domesticate them. Over the millennia to come, the aurochs became one of the foundations of modern civilizations, as well as one of man's first experiments with Mendelian genetics. In Europe and India, the aurochs were actually bred right out of existence, giving way instead to the common taurine cattle of Europe and the zebu of India.

THE ANATOMY OF FIVE DIFFERENT CUTS OF BEEF

Filet mignon: The "dainty fillet" as it's known in French is one of the butcher's most prized cuts. Filet mignon is actually just the front end of a larger piece, the tenderloin, a small, snaking strip of muscle on either rear hip of the cow. Because the cut is from a seldom-used muscle, it's one of the most tender pieces of meat on the animal; due to its limited size, it's also one of the most expensive.

T-bone and porterhouse: Can't decide on just one cut? Try a T-bone or a porterhouse. These expensive, large, and delicious steaks contain meat from two of the tastiest cuts of beef: the tenderloin and the strip steak. Both the T-bone and porterhouse come from the short loin and have that recognizable T-shaped bone dividing the two delicious meats. Porterhouses are cut farther back and have larger servings of tenderloin.

Rib eye: Juicy, fatty, and dripping with flavor, the rib eye is a boneless cut from the cow's rib section. Rib eyes contain no eyes; they were traditionally called that to indicate meat from the "eye" or center of the rib. A slice of beef with a rib or two is simply called rib steak.

Popeseye: A Brit butchering of "Pope's eye," these steaks are tender, thin, fast-cooking cuts from the rump—essentially the

MEAT

cow's massive derriere. The cut originated in Scotland and is delicious when pan-fried to a nice buttery brown.

Sirloin: These tasty cuts come from just behind the short loin, from the part of the back just near the rump. Always ask for a *top sirloin*, the choicest part of the sirloin. Compared to the bottom sirloin, deceptively called "sirloin steak," the top sirloin is leaner, smaller, more tender, and more expensive.

> **MEDIUM RARE** A steak is defined as medium rare when the center of the cut reaches between 130 and 135 degrees Fahrenheit.
>
> **MEDIUM** The ideal doneness for marinated, less expensive steaks is medium. The center of the meat should reach between 140 and 150 degrees Fahrenheit.

Grilled

Chomping into that perfectly charred steak fresh from the grill is one of the greatest feelings known to modern man. The trick to grilling the perfect steak begins with choosing the perfect cut. And marble cuts, such as the rib eye, are among the best for grilling.

Just before putting your steak on the grill, flavor it with a thin coat of olive oil (to give it that perfectly charred appearance) and liberally sprinkle it with salt and pepper. For a perfectly seared, tender steak, the grill should be hotter than hell but with no licking flames. Cook the steak to your desire, remove it from the grill, and let it sit for a couple of minutes to allow the inside juices to open. Then devour. **Preferred cuts:** rib eye, round, top sirloin, filet mignon.

Dry-Marinated

If you don't want to spend a day's earnings on a single meal but you still want to cook an impressive steak, try marinating a cheap cut like skirt steak. You can soak your steak in a favorite marinade, but an increasingly popular method is to dry-marinate the steaks in salt.

To prepare, simply coat both sides of the steak in an avalanche of salt. Seriously, a lot of salt. Let it sit for an hour for every inch of the steak's thickness, at which point the salt will have brought the steak's internal juices to the surface. Now simply rinse the salt off the steak, pat thoroughly dry with a paper towel, and either grill or pan-cook it. **Preferred cuts:** skirt steak, sirloin, flank.

Pan-Seared

The trick to a perfectly seared steak? Quick and hot. Cooking the steak on the highest heat possible will allow the surfaces to get nice and crispy while the interior remains juicy and pink. You can use a good grill, but many top chefs actually prefer to pan-sear a nice cut of meat since the flat pan helps create an even, crispy crust that traps in the flavor.

For the ultimate pan-seared steak, begin by placing your favorite cast iron pan (sans the steak) in the oven and heating

HOW TO PROPERLY COOK A STEAK
Four Incredible Methods for Preparing Beef

As descendants of skilled, savage hunters, we have a biological need to sink our teeth into a sizzling-hot hunk of fresh meat. Even if you don't spend a lot of time cooking, manning the grill is a man's rite of passage. But what's the correct way to prepare a steak? Should you season it? And how cooked should it be? Well, that all depends on several factors, including your personal taste, the cut of meat you choose, and whether or not you have a grill.

TWO RULES OF COOKING STEAK
Never cook it cold. Always let the steak warm up to room temperature. A steak straight from the fridge simply won't cook evenly.

Rare, medium rare, or well done, it's up to you. Unlike other meats like pork or chicken, beef is pretty safe to eat raw as long as the exterior has been cooked. As a rule of thumb, the rarer the center of the steak, the juicier, more tender, and more flavorful it will be.

it to 500 degrees Fahrenheit. Transfer that super-heated pan to the stovetop (use an oven mitt) and turn the heat up to the maximum. Lay your steak in the sizzling-hot pan and sear each side until you get a nice, golden-brown crust (about thirty seconds per side). Turn off the stove and return the pan (this time with the steak) to the 500-degree oven to let the inside cook, around two minutes for medium rare and three minutes for medium. **Preferred cuts:** rib eye, strip, tenderloin.

Broiled

Broiled steaks are a great option…if you have a great broiler. Professional steakhouses use really hot broilers—some can get as hot as 1,800 degrees. Chances are your broiler doesn't do that. Still, a home-broiled steak can be delicious, especially if you have a nice porterhouse or T-bone.

Begin by brushing a fine coat of olive oil onto the cut and then preheating the broiler to the highest setting. Place the steak in a cast iron pan (or, for that barbecue look, a roasting rack) and toss it in the oven, about four inches from the broiler. After about four minutes, remove the steak, throw on some salt and pepper, flip it, and return it to the broiler for another four minutes or so. Done. **Preferred cuts:** porterhouse, T-bone, top sirloin.

TAKING THE ANIMAL OUT OF THE MEAT

When the French Normans conquered England in the eleventh century, they put the English-speaking Anglo-Saxons to work in the fields to oversee their livestock while the French simply *ate* the meat. Today, we still refer to living animals by their English herdsman names while using words of French origin to speak about edible meat. For those who need a quick primer, here's a breakdown of several animals and their corresponding culinary names:

Cow/Beef (French *bœuf*)
Pig/Pork (French *porc*)
Young cattle or calf/Veal (French *veau*)
Sheep/Mutton (French *mouton*)
Chicken/Poultry (French *poulet*)
Deer/Venison (French *venaison*)

The word "venison" originally came from the Latin word *vēnor* ("to hunt") and was used for the meat of any hunted animal, including deer, hare, and boar.

One of the main reasons the French began naming their meat differently from their animals was that it removed the guilt and unpleasantness of consuming once-living flesh. We've continued this tradition in English with terms like Rocky Mountain oysters (deep-fried calf testicles) and sweetbread (cow pancreas or throat). *Bon appétit!*

THE MANual

PORK

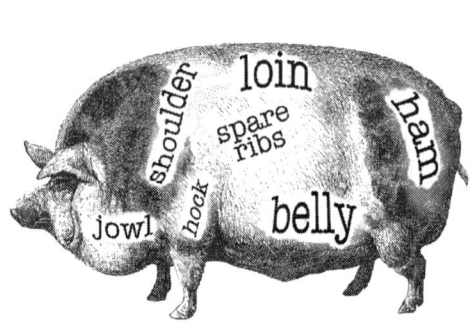

Incredibly, dogs are the only animal in the world to have been domesticated before the pig. Intelligent, sociable, and delicious, Eurasian wild boars were a natural choice to be brought into the fold of human civilization. Like the dog, the exact story of the domestication of pigs is lost to the fact that nobody bothered to take notes during prehistory, but what we do know is that settlers throughout Eurasia began effectively herding and keeping wild boars more than 9,000 years ago.

As voracious omnivores (literally eating just about anything), pigs proved particularly easy to keep. They would feed as happily on roots and grasses as they would discarded meat and fruit. Before long, the domestication of pigs spread throughout Asia, Europe, Polynesia, and Australia, arriving in the Americas in the 1500s alongside the Conquistadors. A testament to their immense popularity, the pig, whose ancestors' population was once limited to a small region of the world, has become one of the most common mammals on earth with an estimated population of over 990 million.

Beware the Pork Curry

Think septic tanks are foul? They have nothing on the **pig toilet**. An efficient and common form of latrine used in China and India for nearly 2,000 years, the pig toilet is pretty much exactly what it sounds like: an outhouse that funneled waste directly into a pig trough. Hungry pigs will apparently eat just about anything. And considering what those pigs were used for, apparently so will people.

 THE MANual

CHICKEN

From Junglefowl to Yardbird

It sounds odd, but the story of the average country chicken starts way out in the hot jungles of southern Asia. That's where the red junglefowl, the domestic chicken's direct ancestor, had made its home for thousands of years when humankind wandered into the Asian subcontinent. The birds lived a quiet existence in their native habitat, feeding on insects, seeds, and fruit. They hardly flew in the dense jungles, taking to the air only in order to roost in the trees or escape momentarily from ground-based predators.

MEAT

Then, at least 5,000 years ago, the early inhabitants of southern Asia started snapping up the junglefowl and keeping them close by. A beautiful, savory relationship began. The junglefowl would provide humans with eggs, meat, and entertainment in the form of cockfighting; in return, human settlements provided an ample supply of seeds and insects, as well as protection from predators.

By the fifth century BC, the domesticated junglefowl had spread throughout the Mediterranean, from Egypt to Greece and from Mount Zion to the Iberian Peninsula. Which means people have been cursing crowing roosters at dawn for a very long time.

LORDS OF THE FLIES

The Hawaiian island of Kauai is overrun by what appears to be red junglefowl. But, while the ancient Polynesians carried domesticated birds across the Pacific, today's wild brood is actually just modern chickens gone feral. After Hurricane Iniki slammed into the island in 1992, hundreds of chickens broke free of their coops and spread out over the island.

Drinking with Hemingway

BOOZE AND BOXING

Ernest Hemingway was a man. He hunted wild game in Africa, drank absinthe in Paris, and ran with the bulls in Pamplona. He wore a respectable mustache. Enjoyed a well-fought boxing match. When he was seventeen, Hemingway adopted the writing style of the first newspaper he worked at and then never gave it up. For that steadfast dedication to clean, crisp writing, he was awarded the Nobel Prize for Literature. In the sixty-one short years before he shot himself, Hemingway had four wives. Yes, Ernest Hemingway was a man.

Ernest Hemingway served in World War I even though the United States was not yet a belligerent. He took jobs as a war correspondent first during the Spanish Civil War and then throughout WWII. At the Liberation of Paris, he was awarded the Bronze Star just for showing up. Yes, Ernest Hemingway was a man. And that should be celebrated. Here are two of his favorite subjects: booze and boxing.

EVERYMAN'S DRINK: BEER

"Beer is proof that God loves us and wants us to be happy."
—Benjamin Franklin

Birth of the Brewski

Around the advent of agriculture, we humans discovered one very important lesson: pretty much any starchy substance with sugar, when exposed to natural yeasts found in the air, will start to gloriously ferment. And that happened a long time ago. In the Fertile Crescent of Mesopotamia, there's evidence that a beerish drink was produced and consumed as far back as 6,000 years ago.

In his book, *The Complete Guide to World Beer*, author Roger Protz echoes numerous anthropologists when he says, "When people of the ancient world realised they could make bread and beer from grain, they stopped roaming and settled down to cultivate cereals in recognisable communities." In other words, not only is beer as old as civilization itself, it helped create the frickin' thing.

Beer then spread to any society that was growing any cereals at all—the ancient Greeks taught the Romans, and the Gauls, Barbarians, and Egyptians were all drinking homemade brews as well. And, like the great modern culture of microbrewing, every taste was different.

By the time 1000 AD rolled around, one big advancement had been made—the addition of hops, a flower growing on the Humulus vine. Hops helped to add flavor and aroma to beer in addition to helping preserve it for future consumption.

Then, at the end of the fifteenth century, man made one giant leap for beerkind: beer-making was taken out of the home and put in the hands of budding professionals. (Considering the number of DIY beer kits now available, apparently we've regressed.) A lot of these newfangled microbreweries were housed in monasteries, where monks worked tirelessly to perfect the art of brewing in order to keep the monasteries in diamonds, furs, and cloaks. So the breweries grew and a golden era of beer innovation began.

The Surprisingly Limited Origins of Beer

Rest, my Precious

The term "lager" (from the German *lagern*) means "storehouse" and comes from the frigid breweries of southeast Germany where brewers were forced to store barrels of fermenting beer for up to a month—instead of the normal week—because the low temperatures hindered yeast growth. Fortunately for the brewers, the wait was worth it as the slow-fermenting beer turned out (arguably) better brews.

Getting pissed on the Thames

Porters, England's stout ales, were named for London's river porters among whom the high-alcohol brown ales were especially popular.

Guinness actually is good for you

All the way up until the Industrial Revolution, beer was one of the primary sources of vital nutrients and vitamins for the underclass in Europe.

THE MANual

> "A fine beer may be judged with only one sip,
> but it's better to be thoroughly sure."
>
> —*Czech saying*

It's the water

In the rough-and-tumble cities of medieval Europe, drinking groundwater was a sketchy proposition (i.e., you could easily get cholera and die). Instead, parched citizens of all ages relied on clean, refreshing ale to stay hydrated.

The battle for the manliest beer

Samuel Adams Utopias is a consistently produced ale so strong (54 proof or 27 percent alcohol by volume) that thirteen states consider it too manly for sale. Where it is sold, patrons can purchase a bottle for a mere $150.

However, a Scottish artisanal brewery called BrewDog absolutely demolished Utopias' paltry accomplishment with their limited edition brew called The End of History. Served in taxidermy roadkill and coming in at a whopping 110 proof, The End of History is by far the most epic beverage ever manufactured. The twelve furry bottles (seven were stuffed into weasels, four into squirrels, and one into a rabbit) sold for $765 each.

RAUCOUS BACCHUS: WINE

Considering the ease with which the sugars in fruit will ferment, the real history of wine probably goes back to our prehistoric ancestors who most likely got hammered on fruit mush in their caves after long days of hitting mammoths with sticks. But even wine as we know it today dates back an impressive 8,000 years. Back in the day, before humankind had even discovered writing, we discovered grapes.

The greatest thing about grapes is that they're basically their own naturally pre-packaged alcohol factories. Not only is the grape easily pressed, but it has a lovely thin skin that carries around its own yeast for fermentation. So even in the earliest grape-blessed civilizations, all you had to do was walk out of your hut, grab a couple bunches from the field, mash them up in a pot, and let nature work its magic.

The only issue was that grapes are notoriously hard to grow. The same thin skin that made them so mashable also made them extremely vulnerable to changes in climate—grapes were killed by heat, frost, mold, insects, and even sunburns. Cultivating grapes became an art form limited to a couple regions around the Mediterranean and, thus, wine became some seriously upper-class drank. Interestingly, very little has changed between ancient Greece and Rome and modern day America; back then beer was considered the beverage of choice for the masses while wine was a bit snobbier.

> **EVEN THE GODS COULDN'T HANDLE THEIR WINE**
> The Ancient Egyptian god of red wine, Shezmu, was also the god of slaughter, execution, blood, and oil. (Also, inexplicably, perfume.)

If You're Going to San Francisco…Bring Me a Bottle of Pinot

When Spanish monks started establishing Catholic missions up the California Coast, they brought their grapevine clippings with them. Wine was an important part of the Catholic sacrament and getting shipments from Europe to the West Coast of North America was not going to happen. Fortunately for them, it turned out that the coast of California conveniently had the same climate as the best wine-growing regions in the Mediterranean. Unfortunately for the monks, their wine varietals kind of sucked and California's famed wine production didn't begin in earnest until vintners like Robert Mondavi started producing the good stuff in the late 1960s. Today the wine craze has swept over America: You can find wineries in surprising locations from Washington State to New Jersey.

Nine Wine Descriptions You Should Know

Reds

Pinot noir: Native to the Burgundy region of France, pinot noir is a finicky, hard-to-grow grape grown mostly in cooler regions. It is considered one of the finest wine-producing grapes, with a wide variety of flavors and aromas.

Merlot: Originally from France but now grown in Northern California, Chile, and Australia, merlot is a medium-bodied grape with strong hints of cherry and plum.

Cabernet: One of the world's easiest grapes to grow, cabernet sauvignon is a hybrid of cabernet franc and sauvignon blanc. It is dense and peppery.

Zinfandel: Zinfandel, which made its way to the states from Croatia, has flavors ranging from raspberry to pepper.

Chianti: A wine particular to a region rather than a grape, Chianti wine comes from the Chianti region of Italy in central Tuscany. It can be made from a variety of Chianti grapes and is generally aged for at least seven months in oak.

THE FOUNTAIN OF YOUTH?

Red wine contains a compound called resveratrol that has been proven to increase the lifespan of some animals by up to 50 percent. Sadly, in order to achieve the same longevity benefits and live to 150, you'd have to drink about 1,000 bottles every day.

Whites

Sauvignon blanc: With origins in France's Bordeaux region, sauvignon blanc is crisp and refreshing, with flavors ranging from vegetal to tropical.

Chardonnay: Originally from France's Burgundy wine region, chardonnay's flavors range from oaky and lean to sweet and fruity. It is easy to make and is used in many sparkling wines.

Pinot grigio: Also originally from Burgundy, pinot gris or pinot grigio is subtle and crisp. It's basically a white replica of pinot noir.

Riesling: A high-sugar wine from cold-ass Germany, Riesling has a strong, flowery scent.

The World's Most Expensive Wine

The most expensive bottle of wine ever sold, a 1787 Chateau Lafite, auctioned in 1985 for $156,000, which translates today to around $315,000. The winning bidder, billionaire

A WINE FIT FOR A CARTEL

The Corsican wine Vin Mariani had all the characteristics of a truly remarkable beverage. Namely, it contained both wine and cocaine. While everyone else in the 1800s was jazzing up their wines with brandies and bubbles, Signor Mariani spiced his with coca leaves, marketing the invention as the ultimate pick-me-up (which we're pretty sure it really truly was).

Malcolm Forbes (yes, *that* Forbes), was under the still unconfirmed impression that the bottle had once been part of President Thomas Jefferson's personal cellar (the initials T.J. are etched into the side of the bottle). Whether the bottle ever truly belonged to Thomas Jefferson is of no consequence, as Forbes bought the bottle for bragging rights rather than a desire to imbibe: the 200-year-old Bordeaux probably turned to undrinkable sludgy, vinegary crap sometime in the early nineteenth century.

The World's Most Expensive Drinkable Wine

A 1997 Dom Romane Conti consistently sells for about $1,540, making it the world's most expensive drinkable wine. With suggestions of berries and leather and tantalizing undertones of soy sauce, licorice, and flowers, this French red Burgundy is apparently the perfect complement to a good burger.

OPEN A BOTTLE OF THE BUBBLY:

CHAMPAGNE

The accidental innovation that is champagne can be summed up in one phrase: "*Merde*, it's cold!" The Champagne region happens to be in the coldest, dreariest corner of northern France (the annual mean temperature is just 50 degrees Fahrenheit). But that didn't stop the freezing citizens of Champagne from growing wine grapes, as difficult as it was. In fact, the chardonnays and pinots they managed to produce were prized around the country, so wine was big business for these northerners.

The biggest problem they faced was that in order to properly activate the yeast, they needed the warmer temperatures of their cousins to the south. But that didn't stop them from trying. And as they attempted to ferment the wines in the cold, they discovered an unfortunate side effect of chilly yeast—it produces a lot of carbon dioxide. So much CO_2, in fact, that their bottles started busting and every time they opened one up, the wine fizzed and bubbled. It took a while for this new carbonated wine to catch on, but eventually it did, and with serious style.

> Careful, on average, twenty-five people accidentally die each year from flying champagne corks.

Mr. Bubbles

Mr. Dom Perignon, the name synonymous with extravagantly priced bubbly (a magnum of Dom sold for a record $1,000,000 in 2010), was a chubby Benedictine monk from northern France. He is credited with revolutionizing the production of the region's unique white wine, which we know today as champagne.

Leave the Champagne to Your Wife

The "Veuve" in the beloved Veuve Cliquot champagne means "widow" and is named after Barbe-Nicole Cliquot, whose husband died and left her his champagne-producing estate (which she in turn made into an empire).

The Most Expensive Bottle of Liquid Ever Sold

$1,946,417 was the final auctioned purchase price of a bottle of Henri IV Dudognon Heritage Cognac Grande Champagne.

 THE MANual

THE FASCINATING HISTORY OF SPIRITS

If the liquor aisle is any indication, it would appear that man can distill just about anything. Vodka is made from potatoes or grain; gin from berries; tequila from succulents; rum from sugar; whiskey from barley; bourbon from corn, and soju from rice. This human ingenuity—actually more of a parched thirst for something boozy—has led to some lip-smacking drinks, hair-burning shots, and downright fascinating events in history.

> *"I should never have switched from scotch to martinis."*
> —*Purported last words of Mr. Humphrey Bogart*

Bartending Terms You Should Know

Call drink: A two-ingredient beverage like Jack and Coke (the term "cocktail" refers to a drink with three or more ingredients).

Neat: Served alone in a glass with no ice.

Nip: One quarter of a liquor bottle.

On the rocks (or over): Served over ice.

Shooter: A straight shot (neat).

Straight up (or up): Shaken (or stirred) with ice and then strained into a glass.

Tot: A small serving of liquor.

Twist: A lemon peel.

Virgin: Something you should never order.

Well drink: A drink made with an unspecified brand of liquor, usually the cheapest swill and normally pretty crappy.

The Green Fairy

Like all respectable liquors, absinthe was originally peddled as medicine. Toward the end of the eighteenth century, Dr. Pierre Ordinaire concocted a "healthy" digestive aid made from three garden herbs—grand wormwood, green anise, and sweet fennel—distilled to a powerful proof, giving absinthe its traditional kick. Dr. Ordinaire then sold his recipe to two sisters in Couvet, Switzerland, who continued to sell small batches of absinthe as medicine.

When a man named Major Daniel Henri Dubied approached the sisters with interest in buying the recipe, absinthe was once again passed along. It was with Major Dubied and his son-in-law Henri-Louis Pernod that absinthe first started really flowing. They built two large-scale distilleries, starting two linked brands of liquor: Dubied Pere et Fils of Switzerland and, the more famous French brand, Maison Pernod Fils.

 THE MANUAL

In the 1840s, France invaded Algeria and the French troops were issued bottles of absinthe as a malaria preventative. When they returned to Paris, they brought a developed palate for the distinctive drink, nicknamed the Green Fairy, and absinthe quickly became the beverage of choice at Parisian bistros and cafés.

Absinthism

By the end of the nineteenth century, absinthe had been vilified. The reason given by quack scientists was the wormwood. Though wormwood had been used since antiquity as a medicinal herb, the presence of a powerful chemical compound known as thujone quickly gave it a false reputation as a highly addictive hallucinogen (it's not). Enjoyers of absinthe quickly found themselves labeled with "absinthism," a condition ten times worse than alcoholism. And by the 1910s absinthe was being banned in countries from Europe to North and South America.

Today, absinthe is once again legal throughout the world, although the recipe no longer reflects that of Dr. Ordinaire.

> While very high proof, several of absinthe's herbal ingredients have stimulant properties that counter the depressant effects of alcohol, leading the drinker to a mentally clear, balanced intoxication experience.

The correct way to enjoy the Green Fairy

Pour one jigger shot of absinthe into a glass. Lay a grated absinthe spoon on top of the glass. Place one sugar cube on the spoon. Pour up to four jigger shots of cold water (to taste) over the sugar cube to dissolve it into the absinthe.

Yo Ho, Yo Ho, a Rum and Coke for Me

Kill-devil be the name, but "rum" got the fame. It was a wicked, blindingly strong drink that put the sailors of the Caribbean in a stupor, earned the name kill-devil, and later became the drink known the world over as rum.

Sugarcane was native to just two places on earth: India and Papua New Guinea. But once the Chinese got ahold of its unique sweetness, sugarcane became one of the most heavily sought-after crops in the world thanks to mankind's natural sweet tooth. It spread everywhere fast. So fast that almost as soon as Christopher Columbus and his crew had set foot on the islands of the Caribbean, they had planted the first sugarcane. Eventually some ingenious European immigrant to the Caribbean started fermenting and distilling molasses—a useless, sugary, nasty-looking byproduct of granulated sugar production—and rum was born.

The image of the rum-guzzling pirate is anything but a myth. In the early days of maritime exploration, stored drinking water would become a slimy, algae-infested mess, so sailors had to devise methods of masking the disgustingness. As first they added wine or beer, but it became unfeasible to meet the

thirsty seamen's needs on longer voyages, so it was replaced with rum.

Rum has been the sailor's drink of choice since 1655, when Britain conquered Jamaica. Rum in its delicious, undiluted form, however, proved problematic, as sailors would often forgo their ration for days on end, opting instead to swill the spirit in excess in one drunken sitting. Among other obvious problems, this tendency caused unacceptable dehydration.

Grog was the solution. Originally referring to watered-down rum (and now a variety of rum-based drinks), this lower proof intoxicant was hydrating as well as enjoyable, and became the beverage of choice for sailors the world over. By the mid-1700s, some admirals and captains tossed lime juice into the mix, and the boost of vitamin C could ward off scurvy (although it usually became oxidized and therefore ineffective). By 1756, grog was deemed so *healthy* that Britain's Royal Navy actually mandated that their sailors drink grog twice daily, and this awesome grog-drinking requirement was practiced all the way up to 1970. So next time you head out on a cruise, make the healthy choice by drinking rum with every meal.

Cap'n Rum

The liquor business has demoted Sir Henry Morgan. Better known as Captain Morgan, Henry Morgan actually retired from Jamaica-based privateering a full admiral in the English Royal Navy.

The Beautiful Blue Agave

> *"One tequila, two tequila, three tequila, floor."*
> —George Carlin

It's hard to fathom just how far men will go for a glass of booze until you know the story of tequila. The farther into Mexico the Spanish Conquistadors got, the lighter their casks of brandy became, until one day their Central American party dried up altogether. Desperate for anything they could ferment and shove down their throats in the middle of the desert, the Spaniards turned to a harsh, booze-like drink that the native inhabitants imbibed, called *pulque*, made from the heart of the blue agave plant. Not caring to waste their time on the low-alcohol content of *pulque*, the Spaniards began distilling the fermented juice into the New World's first native spirit.

The MANual

WHISKEY 101

By the end of the fifteenth century AD, the process of distilling fermented grain had arrived in Britain, Scotland, and Ireland. Undoubtedly the islands erupted in celebration. And Scotch whiskey in its earliest form was a pretty simple no-brainer—Scotland already had plenty of barley fields being used for bread and ale production, so the only piece of equipment needed was a still.

Whiskey production ramped up in Scotland throughout the Renaissance, with small distilleries opening up in nearly every village from Edinburgh to Elgin. When the British government took control of its northerly neighbor in 1707 and saw how profitable the liquor had become in Scotland, they decided they wanted in and started taxing the crap out of it. But if we've learned anything from William Wallace, it's that the Scots take orders from nobody. Instead of paying taxes on the booze, they simply took it underground and started

UISGE BEATHA

In Gaelic, whiskey is called *uisge beatha*, or the "water of life." The name comes from the early medicinal form of the beverage and Latin name *aqua vitae*. The funny thing is, *uisge beatha* deserves the title: recent studies have shown a shot of Scotch has more life-preserving antioxidants than a glass of wine.

smuggling moonshine from one end of the country to the next in such quantities it nearly put the few remaining legal distilleries out of business.

Across the Atlantic to Add an "E"

America has always been seen as the Land of Opportunity, and for Scottish and Irish distillers struggling to make money in a sea of native whiskey (or "whisky," as it is spelled in Scotland and Canada), the New World colonies looked like a great place to ply their trade. When they arrived across the Atlantic, the distillers made straight for the hills and ran into a monumental problem: Barley doesn't grow well in the harsher North American climes. Not to be deterred, the distillers simply switched from a mash made of barley to one made of rye and American rye whiskey was born.

The House of Bourbon

By the end of the eighteenth century, distillers had made it out to the newly declared state of Kentucky, a wild and rural stretch of land that had, until the Revolutionary War, been Indian territory. In order to honor France's help in the recent revolution, a large portion of northern Kentucky was named Bourbon County after Louis XVI's Royal House of Bourbon. Somewhat ironically, what the whiskey makers discovered in Bourbon County was a very similar soil to the best French wine-producing regions and one of the holy grails of alcohol production—pure alkaline waters filtering through the limestone rocks of the Blue Hills.

Because native corn grew so well west of the Allegheny Mountains, it quickly surpassed rye for the production of mash in the recipe, and charred oak barrels were introduced to give the corn whiskey a smooth, woody flavor and its distinctive amber color. Shortly after, the whiskey producers of Bourbon County started shipping vast quantities of the drink down the Mississippi to New Orleans in barrels emblazoned with the point of origin, giving birth to the world-famous name.

Anatomy of a Bourbon

No, it does not need to come from Kentucky to be called bourbon. Actually, carrying that hallowed title only takes the following characteristics:

- At least 51 percent corn mash
- Aged in a new, American, charred white-oak barrel
- Entered that barrel at no more than 125 proof
- Bottled above 80 proof
- Made in America

The term "sour mash" refers to the process of transferring the yeast from one batch of whiskey to the next when fermenting the liquor in order to keep the taste consistent from barrel to barrel.

Between the Rocks and a Hard Taste: The Correct Way to Drink Whiskey

Drinking whiskey on the rocks dulls the taste, but taking it neat dulls the taste *buds*. The proper way to imbibe whiskey is with just a splash of pure mineral water. (Drinking it with Coke just makes you look ridiculous.)

The Holy Ghost

The alcohol content in whiskey is so high that it quickly loses volume to evaporation. This significant loss, known as "the angel's share," makes an old batch of whiskey extremely rare.

A Costly Scotch

In 2005, a bottle of Dalmore 62 Single Highland Malt Scotch Whisky that had been bottled in 1943 and made from a blend of aged single malts sold at an auction for the ridiculous price of $58,000. The jubilant new owner was in a good mood—he promptly opened the rare scotch and enjoyed it with his companions.

A Whiskey Worth its Weight in Gold

Macallan Fine and Rare Collection: no diamonds, no fluff. Just a bottle of good, rare whiskey. It sold for $38,000 in 2005.

ETHANOL MISCELLANEA

Regional vs. Generic

Generic
Mezcal: Fermented blue agave

Regional
Tequila: Mezcal from slopes of the Tequila Volcano in Jalisco, Mexico

Generic
Brandy: Distilled wine

Regional
Cognac: Brandy from the Cognac region of western France

Generic
Whiskey/whisky: Fermented barley, corn, or rye

Regional
Scotch: Malt barley whiskey (peat smoke optional) from Scotland

Regional
Bourbon: Corn mash whiskey from the United States

Whisky or Whiskey?

Without the "e," "whisky" refers only to the Scotch and Canadian varieties. "Whiskey" refers to the Irish and American drinks.

The London Gin Plague

Here's something ironic: The juniper berry, the key ingredient in gin, was originally used to ward off the bubonic plague, but it was the fermented version of the berry that ended up being the real epidemic. During the mid-eighteenth century, cheap gin flowed through London like soiled rain water in the gutters, turning huge swaths of Britons into fall-down drunks. The alcoholism in London got so bad that the city's birth rate actually dropped below the death rate and an entire city began to drink itself to death.

The World's Hardest Drinkers

The Republic of Moldova is a very impoverished Eastern European country that, according to a recent study, is home to the world's heaviest drinkers. The study found that, on average, adult Moldovans consume the equivalent of 18.2 liters of pure ethanol every year, the equivalent of 900 beers or roughly three a day. A good chunk of that consumption comes from bootleg liquor: homemade wine and vodka. Eastern Europe in general accounted for most of the drunkest countries, with the Czech Republic, Hungary, Russia, Ukraine,

 THE MANual

Estonia, Andorra, Romania, Slovenia, and Belarus rounding out the top ten. For those keeping score at home, America isn't even in the top fifty. Drinking around 9 liters per year, we have a lower annual drinking average than Korea (a surprising fourteenth on list with 14.80 liters consumed annually).

> *"Only Irish coffee provides in a single glass all four essential food groups: alcohol, caffeine, sugar, and fat."*
> —Alex Levine

> *"It takes only one drink to get me drunk. The trouble is, I can't remember if it's the thirteenth or the fourteenth."*
> —George Burns

> *"I only take a drink on two occasions— when I'm thirsty and when I'm not."*
> —Brendan Behan

> *"Alcohol may be man's worst enemy, but the bible says love your enemy."*
> —Frank Sinatra

ALL MIXED UP: COCKTAILS

Until Prohibition made liquor illegal, the popularity of cocktails was pretty low. But as soon as the Eighteenth Amendment was ratified, speakeasies everywhere started crafting up new ways of illicitly getting drunk. The main reason for the fancy cocktails? The illegal liquor flowing in America was of somewhat questionable quality, so it was best to hide the booze in a blend of other ingredients. Although many cocktails originated in illegal saloons in America, the drinks became very popular in Europe as they were introduced by expatriate American bartenders who flocked to London and Paris.

The Oldest Cocktail in the United States

America's oldest cocktail is widely regarded as the Sazerac. Invented in New Orleans well before the Civil War by a man named Antoine Peychaud, the drink was named after his favorite brand of cognac, Sazerac-de-Forge et Fils. The Sazerac earned its true popularity when, in 1870, a popular bartender by the name of Leon Lamothe tweaked the recipe to include rye whiskey and absinthe. When absinthe became illegal, additional bitters were substituted to mimic the taste.

But now that you can once again enjoy absinthe, we highly recommend the original recipe: one shot of American rye whiskey, a half shot of absinthe, two dashes Peychaud bitters,

sugar cube, and a twist of lemon. Serve straight up (shaken over ice and strained) in a highball glass.

Two Drinks Courtesy of Ernest Hemingway

"Always do sober what you said you'd do drunk. That will teach you to keep your mouth shut."
—*Ernest Hemingway*

Death in the Afternoon

Hemingway could drink. If you need any proof of that, savor three to five of these absinthe-infused cocktails in one sitting (per his instructions) and see how you hold up. It's like a mimosa on steroids and it'll knock you clear off your seat.

Pour one shot of absinthe in a champagne glass; fill the rest with champagne.

Death in the Gulf Stream

Once you've had your near-death in the afternoon experience, revive yourself with Hemingway's patented pick-me-up from his absinthe days in Paris.

Ingredients: three dashes of Angostura Bitters, one shot of lime juice, one lime peel, two shots of gin. Serve straight up.

In Russian, vodka means "little water."
For that, Russia, we salute you.

And You Thought Grey Goose was Expensive

At $10,000, the Algonquin Hotel martini is one of the most expensive cocktails in the world. The reason it's so expensive? It's served on the rocks. Or, rather, a single big, fat, 1.52-carat diamond rock. The patron has to place the order at least 72 hours in advance to allow a hotel minion time to run around New York City and track down the diamond.

If $10,000 isn't boss enough for you, there's a beverage sold at London's Movida nightclub for $71,000 (35,000 British pounds). It's made with Louis XII cognac, Cristal Rose champagne, and a garnish of edible flakes of twenty-four-carat gold leaf. Like the Algonquin Hotel martini, this beverage is also served on ice: a blinged-out eleven-carat white diamond ring, to be precise.

Two Other Drinks Thanks to the Lost Generation

The Sidecar

As the story goes, a WWI US Army captain with a penchant for drink frequented a small bistro in Paris, arriving there daily in the sidecar of his military-issued motorcycle. When the captain fell ill with a cold, the bartender whipped up this new drink to give him a boost. Come on, it's not that far-fetched. It does have a lot of vitamin C.

> **Death by Liquor**
>
> As fun as drinking is, it is more dangerous than either AIDS or malaria. Drinking causes 2.5 million deaths per year.

Ingredients: one shot cognac, one half shot Grand Marnier, one half shot fresh lemon, lime, or orange juice. Stir and imbibe.

French 75

The first Howitzers were impressive guns and the French 75mm field gun from WWI was a jaw-dropping anti-personnel weapon worthy of a raised glass or two. Or three.

Mix one shot gin with one half shot fresh lemon juice in a champagne glass. Fill the rest with champagne.

SOMETHING TO GO WITH YOUR DRINK?

The Proper Way to Smoke a Cigar

Let's get one thing clear: smoking does not make you manly. Cigarettes dampen your sex drive and your athletic prowess, shorten your already too-short life, and even accelerate male-pattern baldness. We can all agree that there's nothing manly about being an impotent, bald, dead fatty. But there are times in a man's life where he is expected to smoke a cigar and he is expected to enjoy it. These times include:

1. Before his wedding day
2. At the birth of his children
3. At the birth of his grandchildren
4. On his deathbed (because why the hell not?)

El Puro Nace

Two things of note were discovered in 1492: the New World and cigars. When Christopher Columbus and company arrived in the West Indies, one of the first islands they happened upon was Cuba.

As the story goes, a couple of intrepid crewmembers were sent ashore to make contact with the local inhabitants and found a group of Indians smoking a fragrant leaf rolled up in a cornhusk. One of the sailors named Rodrigo de Jerez gave the cornhusk cigar a try, thus introducing greater Europe to mouth, throat, and lung cancer.

By the early seventeenth century, Cuba was already producing tobacco for export back to Europe and by the turn of the nineteenth century, it had become the island's most lucrative cash crop.

Cigar Terms

Anatomy

Bouquet: The scent of the unlit cigar.

Aroma: The scent of the cigar after you've sparked it.

Barrel: The body of the cigar.

Foot: The smoking end of the cigar.

Cap: The round piece of tobacco at the top of the cigar that holds the wrapper together.

Cuban Orgins

Clear Havana: A cigar made purely in Havana, Cuba.

Habanos S.A.: The chief Cuban cigar manufacturer.

Cohiba: The Taíno Indian word for cigar and the name of Cuba's most famous brand (and Fidel Castro's favorite).

Vuelta Abajo: Cuba's premier tobacco-growing region. Cigars from this region are widely considered the best in the world.

Accessories

Guillotine: A cigar cutter with a single or double blade.

Bullet punch: A cigar cutter that punches a round incision in the cap of the cigar.

Humidor: A climate-controlled box that maintains cigar freshness. The ideal settings for a humidor are 70 degrees Fahrenheit with 70 percent humidity.

Choosing a Proper Cigar

There are three general types of cigars: machine-rolled, hand-rolled, and handmade. Talk to any experienced cigar aficionado and they'll tell you the same thing: the only acceptable cigar choice is handmade.

But what's the difference between handmade and hand-rolled? Handmade cigars are crafted entirely by hand by a master

> **Did You Know?**
> A properly humidified cigar can stay fresh for more than half a century.

cigar roller (the whole "rolled on a virgin's thigh" type deal). A hand-rolled cigar has its filler tobacco made by machine and is then assembled into its wrapper by hand. There's very little difference between hand-rolled and machine-rolled, so don't get duped.

Finally, if you're going to buy a cigar, do it right and purchase it from a tobacconist, not a bodega.

The Five Steps of Smoking a Cigar

Enjoy the bouquet

When you first unwrap your cigar, it's important to enjoy the smell of the unlit cigar. Hold it up to your nose and smell along the entire barrel. Then say something poetic, preferably in Spanish, such as, *"Ah, el primer olor de la tierra fértil después de seis meses en el mar"* (Ah, the first scent of the fertile earth after six months at sea).

Cut the cap

In order to draw smoke from the cigar, you need to open the cap. Don't cut too much or the wrapper will start to fray; cleanly clip just enough of the wrapper to draw smoke. The larger the opening, the more smoke you'll take with each draw.

Don't inhale

Smoking a cigar is not about sucking the smoke into your lungs (you'll cough one up). It's about holding the smoke in your mouth and enjoying the taste.

Take your time

You need to leave enough time between your draws to allow the cigar to cool. If you burn it too fast, the heat will ruin the taste. Take one puff every sixty seconds or so. But don't count out loud.

Put it out

You never smoke a cigar all the way to the end. The last two inches or so will taste like crap, becoming more bitter as it nears the end. When you're done, don't mash it into the ashtray; lay it on the side of the tray and let it burn itself out.

Boxing

 THE MANual

GENTLEMANLY BLOODSHED

A HISTORY OF ORGANIZED FISTICUFFS

"If you ever dream of beating me you'd better wake up and apologize."
—*Muhammad Ali*

Boxing in Antiquity

"Do not challenge me too far with show of fist, or you may rouse my rage; and old as I am, I still might stain your breast and lips with blood."
—*The Odyssey*

Boxing wasn't always the sissy sport it is today; back in Ancient Greece, boxers weren't confined by things like rings, rounds, and time limits. They would fight until one boxer gave up, was knocked out, or, in many instances, died. Boxers were (and still are) a prideful breed, so fights could last for hours—even days—before anybody admitted defeat. If a match started to drag, both boxers could agree to trade blow for blow, eliminating such superfluities as defense, movement, and strategy.

Boxing was introduced as an Olympic sport in 688 BC. As with most events of the ancient Greek Olympics, contestants were pretty much naked, though boxers did wear leather thongs wrapped around their knuckles for protection.

As Rome rose to power, boxing continued to be popular both as a sport and in gladiatorial matches. Bouts between slaves or criminals were immensely popular, at least in part because of the insanely high stakes: they were often fought to the death, while the winner might be granted freedom. For the extra-special wow factor, and to expedite the death process, Romans began to affix razor-sharp metal spikes to the boxer's hand thongs. One variation was the myrmex, which translates beautifully to "limb-piercer."

> ## The Death of Boxing in Rome
> By the late fourth century, Rome's Emperor Theodosius the Great was intent on spreading Christianity throughout the Roman Empire and erasing paganism from the face of the earth. In 391 AD, he issued an edict that forced the closure of all pagan temples, including Olympia, where the ancient Olympics were held. By 394 AD, the Olympic Games in Greece were a relic of the pagan past.
>
> Around 500 AD, Theoderic the Great forbade boxing because of the unchristian damage it inflicted upon boxers' precious faces, which were made in God's image.

Russian Fist Fighting

Russians have been organizing fistfights for centuries. Known simply as Russian fist fighting, the sport has existed at least since the thirteenth century and fights were traditionally held for large congregations—often on ice—during holiday times;

children fought first, followed by teenagers and progressively older contestants. It's unclear if the elderly participated in the title bouts.

While Russian fist fighting included standard one-on-one bouts, it also had a variation known as wall-on-wall fighting, which was fought between teams and could include hundreds of fighters. Each side was governed by a resident badass who was not only their best fighter but also their commander and primary tactician. Teams would fight using "walls" of people, while leaders would hold back until the perfect moment, when they'd rush forward and fire a flurry of heavy punches. Wall-on-wall fighting was like tug-of-war, except the objective was to beat the crap out of your opponent until you forced them out of the designated fighting area.

Prizefighting: Bare-Knuckle Badassery

Modern boxing's predecessor emerged in England in the early sixteenth century in a gruesome, gloveless form known as bare-knuckle boxing, prizefighting, or fisticuffs. As the name might suggest, boxers wore no gloves, which significantly changed the tactics required of a good fighter. A misplaced punch that struck skull instead of face could result in a shattered fist. Parries were more difficult as well, for the same reason. Overall, bare-knuckle boxers were *more* careful and less likely to unleash wild power punches.

BOXING

Although the unspoken guidelines of gentlemanly fighting etiquette (no pulling hair, scratching, biting, hitting below the belt, etc.) were generally observed, early bare-knuckle boxing had no written rules whatsoever. Rounds had no time limit and only ended when a fighter fell, got knocked down, or simply gave up. More importantly, bouts had no round limit, and fights would often last for hours on end. The longest official fight on record lasted six hours and fifteen minutes.

The first official bare-knuckle champion was James Figg, who reigned as champion from 1719 to around 1730, when he voluntarily stepped down. Figg was a multitalented fighter who could open up a bottle of 100-proof whoop-ass with everything from fists to backswords (according to some sources, boxing emerged as practice for fencers). He opened an amphitheater and apparently amassed an unbelievable record of 269 and 1 (although he did tally several of those wins by beating his employees). He is considered the father of modern boxing.

As with most things savage and badass, bare-knuckle boxing was not without its dangers. In one of bare-knuckle's earlier manifestations, bands of giant bruisers would roam England trying to gather crowds and cajole the largest locals into fighting them. Because pugilism had no rules, rings, or time limits, death was not an unlikely outcome. Fighters could die from brain injury, exhaustion, or even by hitting their head on stones or other nearby debris.

> ### THE REBIRTH OF BARE-KNUCKLE
> In 2011, bare-knuckle boxing enjoyed its first sanctioned bout since 1889. Bobby Gunn was crowned bare-knuckle champion of the world after his third round knockout over Richard Stewart.

No Sissy Footing, Boys

The Irish, apparently only interested in the blood and guts of pugilism, created a variation of bare-knuckle boxing known as the Irish Stand Down in which fighters were forbade from maneuvering around the ring. In other words, all they could do was stand still and punch the crap out of each other. It was popular in Irish ghettos throughout the UK and US.

In the USSR, in the early twentieth century, there was a sport known as face slapping, which unsurprisingly consisted of men slapping each other across the face. In 1931, two professional face slappers set a record by slapping one another silly for thirty straight hours. The audience, growing weary and bored, demanded the bloodied slappers finally stop.

Modern Boxing

A document called the Queensberry Rules for the Sport of Boxing, written by a Welshman named John Graham Chambers in 1867, revolutionized the sport by instilling more structure through a set of officially mandated rules and regulations. Now known as the Marquess of Queensberry Rules, the document was the first in boxing to require gloves. It also standardized the parameters to include a 24-foot ring, a three-minute round length, and a fifteen-round limit (reduced to twelve in the 1980s), and introduced the concept of points and developed a clear definition of the term "knockout."

KO vs. TKO

A **knockout (KO)** is called when a fighter, grounded down by a punch (not a trip or a fall), cannot rise to his feet for a count of ten seconds.

A **technical knockout (TKO)** is subjectively called by a referee who determines a fighter to be too injured, delirious, or wimpy to continue the fight.

Death in Boxing

Despite important innovations such as rules and referees and gloves, boxing is still deadly, surprising exactly nobody. When the strongest people in the world are punching each other in the head as hard as they can, accidents will happen. A strong punch or a hard fall can result in brain damage or neck injury, and even when a boxer is able to leave the ring, a bad injury can linger and result in delayed death. To get technical about it, the scientific term for the most common fatal brain injury is acute subdural hematoma.

The Irony of Boxing Gloves

Boxing gloves were originally designed to protect the puncher's hands from breaking. Unfortunately, their remarkable efficacy in protecting the hands allowed boxers to fire punches with more power and reckless abandon, ironically making boxing *more* dangerous by increasing the chance of a fatal blow.

Even if you manage to make it through every fight without a death-inducing injury, you may still be screwed. In about twelve to sixteen years, boxing's ghosts could rear their ugly heads in the form of dementia pugilistic, a variation of dementia caused by repeated concussions that afflicts about 15 to 20 percent of professional boxers.

According to a study on deaths of boxers, perhaps as many as 1,355 boxers have died due to injuries since 1890. Of these, head and neck injuries accounted for about 80 percent, though a surprisingly large percentage of these injuries came from falls or what the study labels as "misadventure," which means nobody knows where the hell the brain injury came from. Other deaths occurred from heart failure, infected injuries, a ruptured spleen, and once, according to the study, too much ice water.

Boxing is so dangerous that several health organizations, including the American Medical Association and the medical associations of Britain, Canada, and Australia, have called for a worldwide boxing ban.

A Round Too Many

In 1982, Duk Koo Kim, a South Korean boxer, died four days after suffering a coma-inducing subdural hematoma in a boxing match against fellow lightweight Ray Mancini. Kim's mom, who flew out to see her son while in a coma, took her own life later that year. The referee of the fight also took his own life less than a year after the tragic fight.

According to reports, Kim suffered his hematoma in the fourteenth round from a single punch. Until that point, the match had been incredibly even and well fought.

Kim's death spurred several changes aimed at helping protect the boxer's safety, including reducing matches from fifteen rounds to twelve. Pre-fight medical checks were also vamped up to include brain and lung tests, among other precautionary examinations.

THE ANATOMY OF A JAB

The jab, the most common punch in boxing, is the most important tool in your boxing tool shed. While it's kind of wimpy compared to other blows, it's safe, simple, and effective. You can use it defensively, either to keep an opponent at a distance or parry his punches, or in an offensive combo by following it with a more powerful punch such as a hook or a cross.

Stand

To fire a jab, begin by getting in your natural boxing stance. Your legs should be about shoulder width apart, with one leading foot, and your elbows should be tucked in. Remember! Lead with your off foot (i.e., your left, if you're right-handed).

Extend

Extend your leading arm towards your target, be it a nose, chin, gut, or, if you just found out your girlfriend's been cheating on you, a car window. Chances are you're not going to knock your opponent out with a jab, so concentrate more on speed, balance, and recovery than pure power. Keep your weight centered so that you can quickly fire another punch or defend against your opponent's counterattack.

Twist

As you're extending, your arm should be twisting inward, towards your body, so that when you strike your palm is facing downward. Simultaneously, try to raise your punching shoulder a bit up and in. This will not only provide punching power, but it will have the added bonus of protecting your chin.

Clench

Counterintuitive but true for almost every punch, keep your fist relaxed until just before contact.

 THE MANual

THE ANATOMY OF A LEFT HOOK

The hook can be a powerful weapon, but is also relatively hard to perfect. And while you can fire a hook with either fist, the basic hook is thrown using the leading hand (i.e., your wimpy, weaker hand). A well-delivered hook can result in a knockout. For the purposes of these instructions, we're assuming you're not a southpaw.

The Dipsy-Doo

The hook is sort of like a dance move. It requires dipping, swiveling, and bouncing. From your normal boxing stance, begin with an elegant yet manly dipsy-doo: bend your knees slightly and drop your fist and head a bit to the left.

The Swivel-Bounce-Punch

Bounce back towards the right, swiveling your body as you do so. To increase the power of the punch, lift onto your left toes while digging your right heel into the ground. Remember, this is a manly endeavor: lift onto the ball of your foot, not your tippy toes like some womanly ballerina.

The Punch

Don't forget to punch! If it wasn't already obvious, you should also be firing your punch while swiveling your body. Remember, as always, to keep your fist loose and relaxed until contact. Aim for the jaw or temple—a proper left hook can easily result in a knockout.

The Finish

If you've executed the punch properly, you will only be able to see your stunned opponent out of the corner of your left eye; the rest of your body should be facing to the right.

THE ANATOMY OF AN UPPERCUT

The uppercut, if properly executed, can be among the most devastating blows in boxing or bar fights. A powerful uppercut to an opponent's chin (known to boxers as "the sweet spot") can rattle his soft brain against its rock-hard chamber, making it one of the more effective knockout punches along with the hook and the cross. However, the uppercut is also risky as it takes time to unleash and the mechanics will leave you momentarily exposed to a counterattack.

Get Close

The best uppercuts are those that take your opponent by surprise. Crowd your opponent's body and distract him, perhaps with a flurry of jabs and body blows, or by having your hot girlfriend wink at him from the first row.

Crouch Down

The power of the uppercut comes more from your legs, hips, and torso than from your arms. Bend your knees and get ready to explode into the attack.

Stay Grounded

Contrary to instinct, the most powerful uppercuts are those delivered from a grounded position. Keep your hips low and resist the temptation to jump into the punch.

Twist and Shout

The uncoiling, or torquing of your hips, is the most important part of an effective uppercut. For right-handed uppercuts, lift with your right calf while planting your left heel into the ground. This will naturally cause your hips and shoulders to uncoil, sending a springy force up through your body, through your arm, into your fist, and out through your opponent's cranium. Many boxers find it helpful to release a shout or a grunt to increase passion and power.

Fire the Punch

The trick to a good uppercut punch is to let your arm follow the natural uncoiling of your hips and shoulders. Keep your entire arm and fist relaxed until *just* before impact, tightening at the last possible moment. Remember to aim for the chin. The nose and mouth are decent second choices. A punch to the solar plexus or gut will do in a pinch.

Don't Stop to Admire Your Work

Because of the twisting and torquing required, the uppercut is a *huge* risk. If you landed it properly, chances are your opponent's lying in puddle of his own drool and blood. But if you

THE MANual

somehow missed your target or are a noodly-armed weakling, you've left yourself dangerously exposed to a vicious counter-attack. To ensure you have enough time to recover, don't let your fist soar into the rafters. Snap your arm back towards your own chin as soon as possible after impact.

MASTER OF THE UPPERCUT

Michael Gerard Tyson was born in Brooklyn, New York, during the summer of 1966. Three days before his twenty-second birthday, he became the undisputed heavyweight champion of the world. Despite a career that was marred by in- and out-of-the-ring antics, Mike Tyson truly earned his nickname, The Baddest Man on the Planet. Out of fifty-eight career fights, Tyson won fifty times, forty-four of them by obliterating knockout. His secret was a combo body-shot right-hook and right uppercut that turned the lights out on numerous opponents and earned him the title of "hardest hitter in heavyweight history."

FIVE BOXERS YOU SHOULD HAVE HEARD OF

The Galveston Giant

Jack "The Galveston Giant" Johnson was the world's first African American heavyweight champion of the world. In addition to amassing an incredible eighty wins and forty-five knockouts in 114 official career fights, plus about forty or fifty unofficial wins, he was also one of the world's first celebrity athletes and was probably the most famous African American of the early twentieth century.

Johnson was considered a crafty and patient boxer and was famous for teasing and punishing his opponents. He began matches slowly and, in a brazen show of vanity, often chatted up friends and audience members *during* the fights. As the bouts wore on, he actually bothered giving a crap and fought progressively harder with each subsequent round. At the time, white audience members wanted a show, especially from black fighters, and Johnson was more than willing to give them one. He ensured that fights were sufficient in length by carefully eschewing knockout blows until the later rounds. He also held up weakened opponents when the may have otherwise collapsed so he could deliver flurries of painful punches.

Johnson became the world colored heavyweight champion in 1903 when he beat Denver Ed Martin. He held the title for

2,151 days and only relinquished it because he wanted to beat up whites as well as blacks.

During the peak of Johnson's career, African Americans were barred from fighting in the world heavyweight championship bout. But Johnson refused to let racial barriers hold him back: He followed Tommy Burns, the champion at the time, around the globe, purchasing ringside tickets to each of the man's bouts. From this strategic perch, Johnson would hurl taunts and insults at the frazzled champ and, in 1908, Burns succumbed and agreed to fight. On December 26, 1908, Johnson fought Burns in the first-ever biracial world heavyweight title bout. Johnson won the bout after fourteen rounds by referee's decision.

Johnson's title absolutely enraged the white masses, who began rioting across the United States. African Americans rejoiced, viewing the victory as social progress. Time and time again, a new "Great White Hope" emerged from the shadows only to be defeated by Johnson. The animosity towards Johnson ran so deep that James J. Jeffries, a former heavyweight champ who'd retired six years earlier, came out of retirement for what was labeled The Fight of the Century. Though the fight lasted fifteen rounds, it was an easy victory for Johnson, who felled Jeffries twice, forcing him to throw in the proverbial towel.

Johnson lived a colorful out-of-the-ring life, dabbling in amateur automobile racing, and he often bought himself stylish hand-tailored clothing. Johnson also broke the racial barrier in his personal life; in addition to marrying three white women, he showed as much stamina out of the ring as in it, as evidenced by the parade of women that sometimes came in and out of his hotel rooms.

The Real McCoy

"The Kid McCoy," also known less glamorously as Norman Selby, is considered by most the greatest light heavyweight boxer in the history of history. He used an infamous, cat-like "corkscrew" punch (and rough tape around his fists) to slice open his opponent's faces, and used a keen, "scientific" style to accrue a career record of eighty-one wins—fifty-five by knockout—in ninety-six matches.

McCoy was an undersized scrawnster—he probably weighed no more than 160 pounds after a typhoon—but fearlessly fought men twice his weight. He was crowned middleweight champion of the world, but apparently found no joy in the wimpy title, for he never defended it. Instead, the noodly-armed boxer tried his luck against the best heavyweights of the time. Though he never captured the world heavyweight crown, he beat several very good, very large boxers.

But McCoy owes his legacy equally to his wily antics, both in and out of the ring. His boxing arsenal was filled with devious trickery, and he's credited for inventing the "oh-snap-dude-your-shoe's-untied-oh-wait-lookout-I-just-punched-the-crap-out-of-you" trick, which is a mainstay in modern schoolyard tomfoolery. He also beat the reigning welterweight champion by coating his face in flour to give himself a

sickly, pallid appearance, thus luring his opponent into a false sense of security. A more cruel version of trickery, perhaps known as the "watch-out-for-those-nails" ruse, was quite literal: before a bout against a barefoot brawler, McCoy would toss a handful of nails into the ring, and as his opponent hobbled around to avoid possible impalement or tetanus, McCoy would besiege the sap with his signature corkscrew punch.

Outside of the ring, McCoy was known to stir up the occasional ounce of trouble. He was once was ridiculed in a bar because he was so slight that the patrons refused to believe he was truly McCoy. Challenged to a fight by a drunken scoundrel, McCoy easily silenced the rabble-rouser with a swift knockout punch. The snake, upon waking, reportedly muttered, "Oh my god, that was the Real McCoy."

McCoy's acting talents were so good that he took them to Hollywood, appeared in some movies, and befriended some funny guy named Charlie Chaplin. But by the 1920s he was a drunken, horny, impoverished mess.

Always the ladies man (he had ten wives over the course of his life), McCoy wooed a married woman named Teresa Mors. But during her divorce, chaos ensued and tragedy struck when Mors was fatally shot in McCoy's apartment. The subsequent legal proceeding was the OJ Simpson murder case of the 1920s, and the "if the glove don't fit" moment occurred when McCoy and his attorney enacted Mors' last moments by wresting on the courtroom floor. In a split jury decision, he was found guilty of manslaughter.

BOXING

Battling Siki

Born Baye Fall in Senegal in 1897, Battling Siki was an incredible boxer who briefly reigned as the light heavyweight champion of the world and, for one incredible stretch between 1919 and 1922, amassed forty-three wins in forty-six bouts. But throughout Siki's life, racism and hatred overshadowed his in-the-ring success. Critics and media painted him in wild, savage colors, and racist epithets like "gorilla," "chimpanzee," and "child of the jungle" clearly upset Siki. Siki's career was derailed by partying and wild antics and he eventually met tragedy on the streets of New York City.

Siki was only eight when a French dancer saw him sitting by a dock, staring longingly at the boats and ocean. She offered to take him to France and he agreed, though sadly he didn't risk saying goodbye to his family for fear that his patron would change her mind. Under her tutelage, he moved to France, and by the time he was a teenager he was already boxing professionally, though the beginning of his career was unremarkable. During WWI he joined the French forces and for bravery he was awarded the Medal of Honor.

He returned from war a man and quickly rose to the top of the French boxing scene with the abovementioned winning streak. The streak culminated in 1922 in an epic bout against Georges Carpentier, the reigning light heavyweight champion of the world. The classic match (which was incidentally attended by none other than Ernest Hemingway himself) was apparently rigged, but after Carpentier attacked Siki with an unclassy amount of violence, Siki returned in a rage, and in the sixth round landed a ferocious right windmill that knocked Carpentier out cold. However, the ref, perhaps under the influence of bribery as well, claimed Siki had tripped Carpentier and disqualified the Senegalese boxer. Luckily, the three ringside judges overturned the call and Siki was crowned light heavyweight champion of the world.

The success and accompanying media attention, however, proved too much for Siki, whose reign and boxing success was to be short-lived. He embarked upon an epic and very expensive journey of partying, carousing, and world-class tomfoolery. He devoured champagne and absinthe like they were Evian and was regularly seen gallivanting up and down the streets of Paris in a tuxedo and top hat, walking his lion cubs. Yup. Lion cubs. And if those shenanigans aren't convincingly wild enough, he also had two Great Danes, which he trained to perform tricks whenever he fired his revolvers into the Parisian sky.

Siki's partying took its toll and his life quickly spiraled out of control. On St. Paddy's Day of 1922, just a few months after earning the title, he relinquished it to an Irishman named Mike McTigue. Soon thereafter he moved to Manhattan where, despite the existence of Prohibition, he trained while plastered. There are accounts of him brawling his way to freedom after refusing to pay the tab at speakeasies, and others of him sneaking out of taxicabs after long, meandering rides. Siki was teetering on the dangerous edge of revelry, and it caught up to him one night in 1925 when he was found dead with two bullets in his back.

The Black Terror

William "The Black Terror" Richmond, born a slave in Staten Island, gained his freedom during the Revolutionary War when Britain gained control of New York. Lord Percy, the Duke of Northumberland, got to know the fourteen-year-old Richmond, who was charming, quick-witted, and had an amusing knack for mimicry. The Duke asked the young Richmond to be his servant and in 1777 the two of them went to England.

Richmond lived a relatively peaceful and sheltered life in the Duke's household and began working as a carpenter's apprentice. Richmond's fists turned out to be as quick as his wit, though he may have never discovered his talent had racism not run rampant on the streets of London in the late eighteenth century. One day a gutterpunk hurled a racist comment in Richmond's direction, and Richmond responding by hurling a flurry of lightning-fast punches that absolutely demolished the bigot—by some accounts leaving him totally blind.

There were more racists, more derisive comments, and more patented Richmond-style beatdowns. Richmond began to realize that his hands could make more money throwing punches than shaping wood, and so in 1804 the undersized Richmond entered London's pugilistic underground. Despite losing his first bout, he captured the English-speaking world's attention as The Black Terror. At about 140 pounds, Richmond was a welterweight by today's weight classes, but he often fought—and beat—boxers who were more than 60 pounds heavier than him. Oh yeah, and Richmond never received a single boxing lesson.

Richmond's strength was his defense; he was quick and in early rounds would consistently parry or dodge every punch by ducking, slipping, sliding, and countering. In his most famous fight, one for the crown of English bare-knuckle boxing, Richmond went *sixty rounds* against the future world champion Tom Cribb, who was unable to land a single punch in the early rounds. Richmond was technically superior, but after several rounds Cribb's massive size and dominant strength wore Richmond down and he eventually lost.

Unlike most stories in this pervasively tragic list, Richmond's ends happily; at age fifty-two he retired from boxing and used his money to buy a club and start a boxing academy.

Your Body Is Your Temple of Doom

Diseases, Disorders, and
Deformities That'll Make You
Feel Better About Your Life

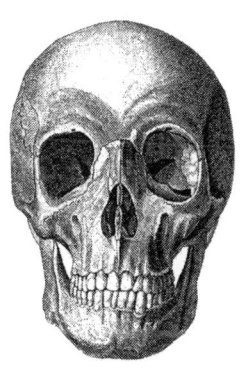

YOU ARE A FILTHY, FILTHY HUMAN BEING

Let's talk about you. By the looks of it, you are a disgusting creature.

During your lifetime, you will produce enough mucus to fill a backyard swimming pool. And you'll produce enough saliva to fill two.

Your tongue is a regular melting pot of life; it can be home to as many as 1,000 unique types of bacteria. That white film on the top of your tongue? That's New York City. Only your tongue's metropolis is made up of tens of millions of living bacteria and dead skin cells. Pride yourself on your oral hygiene? Good for you; your mouth is still dirtier than your toilet seat. Now, don't forget to floss.

Let's talk a little more about oral hygiene. In your mouth, bacteria grow like microscopic weeds. Spend a couple of days not brushing and the 100,000 individual bacteria on each tooth can bloom to ten million. And while most of these bacteria are harmless, plenty of them aren't. Some bacteria found in the mouth are responsible for a ridiculous number of issues that, by all logic, shouldn't be affected by stuff crawling around in your kisser, like heart disease, osteoporosis, and even dementia. All thanks to the warm bacteria that make your mouth smell like a dirty diaper in the morning.

YOUR BODY IS YOUR TEMPLE OF DOOM

Your mouth is dirty, but what about the rest of your body? Glad you asked. You've basically got an entire universe of life in your stomach and intestines, where fifty million bacteria per square inch call home. In fact, the leading danger of the unpleasant intestinal disorder ulcerative colitis is that the plethora of bacteria in your colon might accidentally get released through bleeding ulcers into your normally sterile internal organs.

But don't think that all your bacteria is safely locked up inside your body. Each square inch of your skin also contains over thirty-two million bacteria. It's this bacteria that causes your body to stink when you sweat. And you sweat a lot…up to a pint a day. So, maybe you're using the wrong soap?

Let's back up to thirty-two million bacteria per square inch of skin. You've got a lot of inches of skin on your body. After all, the skin is the largest human organ. And it creates some other headaches. For one, do you think that's dust you're sweeping up every couple of weeks in your apartment? It's not. It's you. Every day you shed 600,000 skin cells. So a lot of that dust covering your floor is actually your former body.

Now that you're sufficiently comfortable with your body, let's spend a quick minute talking about what comes out of it. I'm talking mounting the ivory throne. Heading to the gentleman's office. Clearing some excess inventory. Poop.

Let's start with the fact that you fart an average of fourteen times every day, with some days being more audible than others. Farts are actually harmful to the environment; cows collectively release up to 100 million tons of methane per year through excessive farting, making them the one of the worst emitters of greenhouse gases.

What's more, you are your own little food factory. Of all the food and drink you take into your body, you process only a small percentage into energy (depending on how much fiber you're eating). The rest of it, on average about 400 pounds per year, gets flushed out of your body and into the toilet.

Of course, as it turns out, you're not necessarily the only one getting fed…

YOUR BODY IS YOUR TEMPLE OF DOOM

WORMS. WOOOOORMS. WOOOOOORRRRMMMS.

The Tapeworm: The *Other* Other White Meat

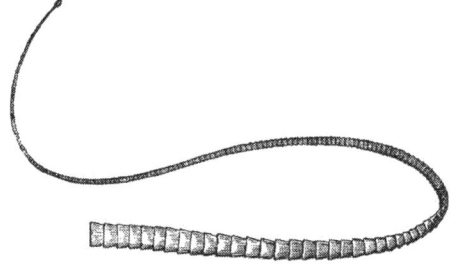

You need to respect tapeworms. They've been around for at least 250 million years and they're not going anywhere. Also, they're huge and hermaphroditic and should rightfully creep you out.

The tapeworm's life cycle is like an odyssey of horrors. It goes something like this: the adult tapeworms drop their ladyboy eggs into the intestine of their host (normally a nice bulky mammalian farm animal) who deposits the eggs through their poop into the same field where all their friends are munching on grass. The baby tapeworms then enter the new host, latching onto whatever fleshy thing they can—muscles, fat, etc. And when that farm animal eventually ends up on your plate

> The longest tapeworm in the world makes its home in the intestines of sperm whales. The whale tapeworm, *Polygonoporus giganticus*, can grow up to 100 feet long.

as a 12-ounce, partially cooked steak, you enjoy every last bite, tapeworms included.

A couple of months later, the tapeworm has latched onto the side of your intestine, sucking vital nutrients from your diet and growing stronger and larger, hoping to one day have some children of its own. When it finally dislodges from your intestinal wall, the tapeworm ends up cruising down your intestinal tract with the rest of your unwanted materials. If you're lucky, you flush it down without noticing. If you're not lucky, you end up giving birth to a three-foot long tapeworm in the middle of what was supposed to be a romantic bath. But, you know, water births are supposed to be really, like, spiritual.

The Pinworm: Check Your Underpants

The pinworm, like its larger, hungrier tapeworm cousin, enjoys a particularly adventurous odyssey through your intestinal tract. The start of the pinworm's story begins when you unwittingly consume it as a wee little egg along with a couple dozen of his sisters and brothers, normally as part of some sort of undercooked meat dish. The eggs are tiny and colorless, so unless you're scanning your meal with a telescope, chances are you're going to be none the wiser.

After your accidental dinner of worm babies, you get to play the role of nurturing incubator while a colony of pinworms blossoms in your small intestine. Here, they hang out, play pinworm games, and grow stronger and larger, eventually feeling bold enough to venture down your gastrointestinal tract.

When they reach your ileum, the last stop in your intestines before the colon, the traveling pinworm colony pauses for a raucous sex party, impregnating all the womenfolk and exhausting all the male pinworms to the point of death.

Finally, in the middle of the night, the pregnant females wriggle their way through the rectum and out your anus, where they drop off their eggs and die. But not before all their wriggling around itches the crap out of you, forcing you to unconsciously scratch your behind, spreading the eggs from your butt to your hand and, eventually, from your hand to your mouth—thus starting the beautiful circle of life all over again.

The Guinea Worm: Let's Hang Out

Of all the parasitic worms in the world, the guinea worm has to be the most panic-inducing. The water- and flea-borne worm is not particularly harmful—the victim's symptoms are normally limited to nausea and mild fever—but when the guinea worm is fully grown—and we're talking three-feet-long fully grown—it decides it wants out of your body and starts painfully pushing its way to one of your feet or arms. When it gets there, the guinea worm starts knocking on your skin, eventually creating an itchy, burning blister that it knows you just can't help but pick at.

When you finally open the blister, the worm sticks its head out, waiting for you to plunge your infected arm into some soothing water, where it will take the opportunity to reproduce. Now you've got the head of three-foot long worm sticking out of your arm. What to do? This is where the situation gets thoroughly suicide-inducing. You can't just pull a guinea worm out of your body; its head will break off, the worm will die, and then its carcass will begin to rot inside your arm. Instead, you have to wrap the head of the worm around a stick and slooowly roll the worm out over a span of up to three months.

GOD-AWFUL PARASITES

Chagas Disease: The Kiss of Death

In the middle of the night, the beetle-like triatomine bug emerges from a crack in the wall of your Cancún hotel room, drops down onto your body, and begins sucking your blood. It's preferred feeding location? Your face. The tendency to face-suck its victims has earned the triatomine the romantic nickname of the kissing bug. But really, it's less like a kiss and more like a Hot Karl, because once its done making out with your cheek it inexplicably takes a crap on your face.

After it's eaten and defecated, the bug moves on, but its poop doesn't. Through all your tossing and turning, the fecal matter eventually finds its way into either the bloody wound or your eye. Unfortunately for you, inside that poop is a really messed-up parasite called *Trypanosoma cruzi* that enters your bloodstream and sets up camp all over the place. Then, nothing happens. For thirty years. You show no weird symptoms (beyond maybe some mild fatigue, body aches, and nausea) and live your life normally until one day, you simply drop dead when your parasite-enlarged heart explodes.

The scariest thing about this disease? A lot of people have it. Chagas disease, as it is called, is endemic to Central and South America and the Center for Disease Control estimates that between eight and eleven million people are living with the disease right now. They just don't know it yet.

Candiru: Worst Frickin' Catfish in the World

Catfish are not the most majestic creatures on planet Earth. They're slimy. They bite. They're freakish bottom-feeders. But none are as savage as the *Vandellia cirrhosa*, the dreaded candiru. This miniscule, parasitic, bloodsucking catfish has a propensity for hiding…in the urethra of human men. You read that right. Do a little skinny-dipping in the Amazon River and you may end up with a miniature catfish in your pee hole. But wait, wait, it gets worse. This devilish little catfish has spiny barbs on its gills that allow the fish to anchor itself in place. And you thought your gonorrhea was bad.

OLD-TIMEY DISEASES THAT STILL WANT TO KILL YOU

Bubonic Plague

It starts with swelling in the worst place imaginable: your groin. Next, painful blisters pop up on your neck and under your armpits. The chills set in and your temperature runs to 103 degrees Fahrenheit. You vomit uncontrollably. And then, when you couldn't imagine the experience getting worse, it does. Gangrene takes over your hands, arms, and feet and your skin begins to painfully rot off while you're still alive. If you're lucky, four days after you noticed your swollen groin, you slip into a coma and die. If you survive, your good looks will have literally fallen off your face.

That was what it was like to contract the flea-borne bubonic plague. And in the Late Middle Ages, the so-called black death swept across the globe with devastating force, wiping out between seventy-five million and 200 million people, nearly a quarter of the world's population and half of Europe.

But the bubonic plague never disappeared; people still contract the plague every year. Most of the time it happens in the far reaches of the world like India or Peru, but in 2012, cases were reported as close by as Colorado and Oregon. Fortunately, the bubonic plague isn't as deadly when treated quickly, killing only a small percentage of those infected.

The Spanish Influenza

While every school child learns about the bubonic plague, the 1918 flu pandemic is one of history's best-kept secrets. Perhaps it's too scary to teach children that something as simple as the flu, in the twentieth century no less, killed as many as 100 million people worldwide in just two years. Whatever the reason, the "forgotten pandemic" was particularly catastrophic since it easily dispatched young, able-bodied men and women in their teens and twenties, a demographic that usually doesn't succumb to the flu.

Symptoms of the flu were god-awful. In addition to the normal fever and body aches associated with the flu, Spanish influenza caused extreme internal hemorrhaging. Blood would pour out of every single one of the victim's orifices—ears, nose, mouth, anus, and even eyes. While the infected often died from secondary infections such as pneumonia, hemorrhaging in vital organs like the lungs could also kill quickly. About one in three people living on earth became infected with the Spanish flu, and between 10 and 20 percent of them died.

How does this affect you in the twenty-first century? Well, the Spanish flu is believed to have been a mutated strain of H1N1—the same form of influenza, better known as swine flu, that killed an estimated 17,000 people worldwide in 2009.

Scurvy

Scurvy isn't just for pirates. The devastating effects of vitamin C deficiency can hit anyone at any time. Aside from unsightly lesions that appear on your arms and legs, the most visible sign of scurvy is that your gums dissolve into a thin, spongy mess and your teeth start to feel looser and looser until they begin falling out. As scurvy progresses, your skin turns a sickly, jaundiced yellow and becomes pocked with oozing wounds that bleed uncontrollably. At the very end, your body becomes wracked with fever and, if left untreated, you die. All because you didn't drink your orange juice.

The problem with vitamin C is that foods chock-full of it—oranges, broccoli, strawberries, etc.—go bad fairly quickly, making them exceptionally difficult to transport, say, on a ship from the Caribbean to the South Pacific. This dilemma left seafarers back in the day with nothing to eat but cured meats, basic grains, and hardtack. Entire crews would often come down with scurvy on long journeys out at sea, only to have to fight to replenish their bodies the moment they hit dry land.

One of the primary groups in danger of developing scurvy today: college students. Close to broke and on their own for the first time in their lives, these poor souls can fall into pathetic vitamin-free eating patterns, just one step away from becoming potheads with dentures.

Sleepy Sickness

Encephalitis lethargica, aka sleepy sickness (aka "Aahh, zombies!!"), raged around the globe right after everyone had just gotten over the Spanish flu. The sweetly named disease came on gently, typically with a run-of-the-mill sore throat, before paralyzing the afflicted person in a completely motionless state; physically frozen, eyes peeled open, and unable to speak. But completely conscious. After recovering (if they did), the patient would display horrific personality defects ranging from psychosis and intense sexual aggression to uncontrollable bouts of shouting.

Although new cases of the disease abruptly stopped appearing in 1928, doctors never figured out what caused sleepy sickness. Or if it would ever come back.

Cholera

For most of us, cholera is something that people died of on the Oregon Trail right after they lost three oxen trying to ford a river. But the disease is actually alive and well. It still affects an average of four million people each year, killing about 100,000 victims annually. The disease, which is caused by the lovely bacterium *Vibrio cholerae*, is transmitted the same way as most other forms of gastroenteritis—via food or water contaminated with the feces of someone who has cholera. Which is scary considering how quickly and viciously cholera epidemics spread. Apparently, it's very easy to eat fecal matter.

Your Body Is Your Temple of Doom

Unlike your traditional stomach flu, cholera is unbelievably powerful. As the bacteria enters your digestive system, it triggers your intestines to drain all of the liquid in your body through your colon, causing gallons of fishy-smelling "rice water" to shoot from your butt. During particularly severe epidemics, victims are lined up in hospital beds covered in plastic with a simple hole and bucket to catch the prolific amount of wastewater. Although cholera is now rarely deadly if treated quickly with fluid and antibiotics, some virulent strains can kill within two hours of the first appearance of symptoms.

Not Your Ordinary Airsick Bag

Some forms of cholera come on so quickly that commercial aircrafts making long-haul flights are still required to carry IV bags in case someone begins showing symptoms mid-flight. Without the emergency fluids, the stricken person could die from dehydration before the plane is able to land.

Syphilis

It did what all the G-men in the country couldn't: took out the notorious gangster Al Capone. No, it's no free-shooting, Thompson-toting, rogue agent; it's the slow and steady sexually transmitted disease syphilis. First noticed at the end of the fifteenth century, syphilis destroys the body in three distinct stages.

First, within a couple days to a few months after one particularly wild night, a few painful lesions appear at the point of contact with the infected host. In case you didn't guess, this is normally somewhere around your private parts. Next, a particularly nasty (but painless) rash spreads over your body. Unfortunately, those are just the overtures. Because somewhere between three and fifteen years after your initial infection, it finally spreads to your central nervous system and your brain, causing violent seizures, tremors, depression, and eventually blindness and dementia.

But don't be fooled into thinking syphilis is a relic of some bygone era. In 2011 alone, the Center for Disease Control estimates there were over 46,000 new cases of syphilis in the United States, nearly the same as the number of new cases of HIV.

Awww, Poor Baby Has the Stomach Flu?

Nope. There's no such thing as the "stomach influenza." The persistent vomiting and diarrhea you are experiencing in front of your girlfriend is caused by a variety of infectious viruses and bacteria conveniently lumped together under the term *gastroenteritis*. In layman's speak, it simply means that you consumed food or water contaminated with infected fecal matter. You ate poop, dude.

Scabies

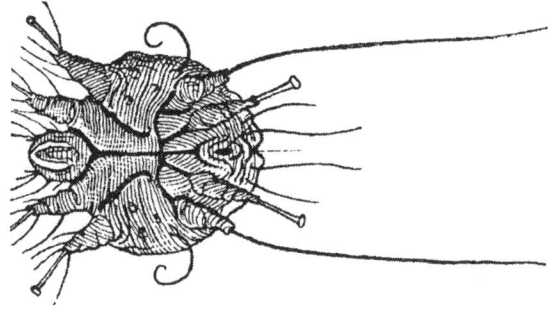

Latin may be a dead language, but its word for "to scratch" lives on in the miniature, eight-legged mite known to scientists as *Sarcoptes scabiei* and to you as scabies. The parasitic mites spread by hot and heavy skin-to-skin contact, but you won't notice for another month or two. First, the female will find a nice location on your skin for a permanent baby-dropping burrow. After digging a warm little hole, she'll begin popping out two or three eggs a day for the rest of her life. These eggs will grow up to be nasty little buggers who love nothing more than devouring human flesh.

While the females spend most of their time relaxing in their cavernous apartments in your skin, the males are out wandering around your body, digging holes and hoping to meet a nice fertile female to settle down with and have more flesh-devouring offspring.

You can actually see the mites' homes: The burrows they've drilled through your skin appear as little pimples. But what's worse is that your body is actually allergic to the mites themselves and, as your immune system tries to attack the scabies, it causes you to itch uncontrollably.

In people with compromised immune systems, the infection can be ten times worse. Mite populations explode and lead to infestations called crusted scabies—covering the entire body in a layer of scabies-encrusted skin.

Smallpox

Here's a scary statistic: Smallpox killed between 300 million and half a billion people in the twentieth century *alone*. If you were to count the infectious disease as a natural disaster alongside earthquakes, tsunamis, and floods, smallpox would be the number-one deadliest natural disaster in history.

One of the most dreaded airborne diseases, the smallpox virus multiplies quickly, spreading through your mouth, throat, and lymph nodes and into your bloodstream about ten days after infection. Eventually it even infiltrates your bone marrow. And the symptoms are swift and brutal. At first you think you've come down with a common cold, but within two weeks your throat and mouth are covered with virus-filled lesions. Once the lesions burst, they fill your saliva with vast quantities of the virus, turning you into a biological weapon.

A couple days after your mouth starts spewing smallpox, it spreads to your face, arms, stomach, and then legs (this is where the *pox*, or "spots," part of the disease comes in) until pretty much every inch of your skin is covered in small, disgusting pimples. While the mortality rate for the impressively deadly disease has only ever been about 30 percent, it left entire populations reeling. And those who survived were often scarred for life by the festering rash.

Although the World Health Organization proudly proclaimed smallpox officially eradicated in 1971, both Russia and the United States kept living samples of the disease. It's just a bad movie script waiting to strike.

YOUR BODY HAS A MIND OF ITS OWN

Exploding Head Syndrome: You Know What? Actually Not as Bad as It Sounds

Despite its utterly terrifying name, exploding head syndrome is entirely mental. It can start up at any point in your life, but usually occurs during times of extreme stress. Just as you're about to enter that nice deep sleep...*BANG!*...you're startled awake by what could only be someone playing the clash cymbals by your head. Only its actually just you hallucinating someone playing clash cymbals, possibly the most annoying hallucination to have right before you fall asleep. Immediately after the head explosion, your heart races, you sweat and curse, and you probably have a pretty tough time getting back to sleep. While the occurrence for most people is rare, some unfortunate dreamers have chronic exploding head syndrome, often leading to an intense phobia of going to sleep. The cure? Relax. Take a vacation.

Alopecia Areata: Hair Today, Gone Tomorrow

Most men curse genetics for their normal bout with male-pattern baldness. But those who suffer from the rare alopecia areata have the real frustration. That's because alopecia areata is totally random. Instead of a handsome horseshoe of hair loss, it happens in clumps, patches, or, in the case of alopecia areata universalis, it happens *everywhere* (eyebrows, eyelashes, chest hair, leg hair: all gone). While the hair can grow back eventually, its reemergence is as random as the hair loss itself.

Acromegaly: Growing and Growing and Growing

As you pass oh-so-gracefully through puberty, your pituitary gland works overtime, secreting the necessary human growth hormone (HGH) to turn you from a four-foot child to a six-foot pimple factory. And at the end of puberty, your pituitary gland shuts down production of HGH and congratulates itself on turning you into a man. But sometimes it starts back up again.

Acromegaly, a form of adult-onset gigantism is one terrifying prospect. It can happen to anyone. Normally caused by tumors on the pituitary gland, the disorder restarts HGH production in your body with a vengeance. And almost overnight you start growing again (and growing and growing). Your hands and face swell and before you know it you have an uncanny resemblance to Andre the Giant. That's what happened to Tanya Angus, a five-foot-eight college student who, at the age of twenty-one, began to transform during a single semester away at school. By the time she died from related heart failure after battling the disorder for over a decade, Tanya's uncontrollable gigantism had taken her from a slender frame to an enormous seven feet and 400 pounds.

> ### Life's Hard for the Big Guy
> John Middleton was an impoverished, nine-foot English giant who, as the story goes, lived in a house so small he had to sleep with his feet sticking out the window.

Lewandowsky-Lutz Dysplasia: Growing Roots

So rare that it's normally referred to by its Latin name, *Epidermodysplasia verruciformis*, this hereditary disease is one of the strangest in the world. The disease, which is caused by the common *human papillomavirus* (HPV), is characterized by the uncontrollable growth of massive warts all over the body. One Javanese man named Dede Koswara developed such an intense form of the disease that his skin and limbs began to resemble the bark and branches of a tree, earning him the nickname Tree Man. The wart growths were so massive that Dede lost use of his hands beneath multiple pounds oversized warts. When Dede finally had an operation to remove the growths, doctors cut off a full 13 pounds of wart-covered flesh. Unfortunately, within a couple of years the growths had returned.

Permanent Insomnia: Sleep When You're Dead

Almost everyone deals with short bouts of insomnia from time to time. Stress, anxiety, upset stomach, and hormonal shifts can all cause restless nights. But, for a very unlucky few, insomnia can become so persistent it becomes permanent.

That's the story of Thai Ngoc, a Vietnamese farmer who, in 1973, came down with a bad fever and reportedly lost the ability to sleep. Despite desperate attempts to get some shut-eye with home remedies, pills, and alcohol, nothing worked for the insomniac. When doctors observed Thai in 2006, a full three decades since the last time he successfully slept, he was miraculously in excellent health. Although he was a little grumpier than your average farmer and had reduced liver function, he showed remarkable energy for a man who hadn't slept in over 10,000 nights. In the ultimate test of a rested man, he could still carry a 100-pound sack of rice for over two miles.

REM Behavior Disorder: Go Live Your Dreams

At the other end of the spectrum from permanent insomniacs, you have the particularly troubling rapid eye movement behavior disorder. This adventurous sleep disorder causes people to act out their dreams as they're happening. For most sleepers, entering the REM cycle of sleep is pleasant, quiet, and full of wild, action-packed dreams. And for most people, the REM cycle comes with REM atonia, the off switch that paralyzes the body so it can't act out the Olympic ski jump happening in a dream. But people lacking that off switch do act out their dreams, turning what was a quiet night into a sleepy ambulance ride to the hospital.

THE MANual

SPOOKY FREAK SHOW DISORDERS

Siamese Nightmare

Conjoined twins are identical twins who joined forces in the embryo, and they can be connected pretty much anywhere—at the pelvis, back, chest, face, or even skull. Most conjoined twins share at least some internal organs, including the heart, making separation a precarious—and often impossible—undertaking.

As you might imagine, conjoined twins have it pretty tough. Only about 25 percent of them survive past infancy, and those who do face a lifelong struggle. Besides the obvious obstacles ("Which way are you walking?" "Can you please make love more quietly?"), conjoined twins suffer much worse burdens that are often particular to the locale and nature of

THE ORIGINAL SIAMESE TWINS

Chang and Eng Bunker, the conjoined brothers born in Siam (now Thailand) in 1811 were the basis for the term "Siamese twins." Connected at their midsection, the brothers each had a full set of arms and legs. They married a pair of sisters who bore twenty-one of Chang and Eng's children between them. Logistics? We want to know too.

their attachment. Parasitic twins—twins whose relationship is asymmetrical—are perhaps the least fortunate, as one is usually smaller, weaker, and completely dependent on their more able twin.

The Elephant Man: Elephantiasis

Elephantiasis, or *lymphatic filariasis* as it's properly known, is spread by a cooperative combination of two unsavory characters: parasitic worms and the mosquitoes that carry them. The worm uses the mosquito as a mail service, getting its thread-like larvae deposited into your skin. From there, the roundworms wriggle through your body, working their way into your lymphatic vessels, where they can thrive for the better part of a decade.

Although the worm is unpleasant, it's not actually what causes your limbs to balloon to the size of an elephant's. The worm is teeming with heavy-duty bacteria that your body tries to attack, causing localized inflammation. As the inflammation builds and backs up, it causes swelling under the skin, creating grotesquely sized body parts—normally around the legs and feet.

For such a disturbingly deformative disease, elephantiasis is remarkably common; it afflicts about 120 million people, primarily in Africa and Southeast Asia.

> ### Hold on, It Gets Worse
> One particular form of elephantiasis, known as scrotal elephantiasis, targets the scrotum alone, leaving the victim to suffer with testicles swollen to the size of a watermelon.

Children of the Night: Xeroderma Pigmentosum

Of all the things you can be allergic to—peanuts, cats, your own semen (it happens)—the sun has got to be one of the worst. But that's what afflicts about one in every 250,000 people around the world. Known as xeroderma pigmentosum, this genetic disorder causes its victims to develop severe sunburns after just a few minutes exposed to sunlight. The disorder also causes the eyes to burn red after any exposure to ultraviolet light, often forcing the victims to live their lives entirely after the sun has gone down, hence the term "children of the night."

YOUR BODY IS YOUR TEMPLE OF DOOM

A Short Guide to Little People

Dwarves: Dwarfism can be caused by over 200 conditions, including basic growth-hormone deficiency, which results in a proportionally smaller person, and achondroplasia, which causes disproportionately short limbs and an abnormally large head.

Primordial dwarves: Primordial dwarves can be even smaller than normal dwarves because they grow at a stunted rate during every single phase of development. At a mere one foot nine, the seventy-three-year-old Mr. Chandra Bahadur Dangi is the shortest adult ever measured.

Midgets: Don't call a little person a midget—it's actually offensive. It means something close to "sand fly" and was used mockingly by sideshow promoters. For a long time it was used to describe proportional dwarves, but today it's essentially a slur.

Little people: People who are abnormally small-bodied prefer to be called little people. Little people are often defined as people under four foot ten.

Pygmies: Although the term "pygmy" is most closely associated with the small hunter-gatherer tribes of central Africa, it actually refers to ethnic groups all around the world, including in Indonesia, the Philippines, Bolivia, and Brazil. In fact, the term refers to ethnic groups where adult males' average height is less than four foot eleven.

Hobbits: Hobbits are fictional, moron. *Never* call a little person a hobbit.

THE REAL HOBBITS

However...about 18,000 years ago, on the island of Flores in Indonesia, a group of very little people flourished. These so-called hobbit people were about three and a half feet tall and shared the island with giant rats, huge lizards, and a species of tiny dwarf elephants called Stegodon.

Nature's Werewolf: Hypertrichosis

Sometimes our body's hair-producing hormones start working overtime, resulting in humans covered in thick coats of fur-like hair. Hypertrichosis can strike in utero, giving infants those classic, adorable full-body beards.

Also known as the werewolf syndrome, the condition has two basic forms; general hypertrichosis results in a monkey-like, full-body coat, while localized hypertrichosis is limited to hairiness in a specific region like, say, the elbow.

Lionel the Lion-faced Man is one of the most famous real-life werewolves. During his heyday in the early twentieth century, the sideshow performer had eight-inch hair dangling from his face and four inches of hair sprouting from pretty much everywhere else.

An Earie Record

Hair in weird places is an unfortunate drawback of virility. Men have more hair than women do on their chests, stomachs, backs, arms, feet, hands, noses, and ears because they naturally have higher levels of a male hormone called androgen.

Under the androgenic hair rubric of manliness, an Indian grocer named Radhakant Baijpai is the manliest of all men. Despite his wife's incessant pleading, Mr. Hadhakant refuses to chop off his gnarly, record-holding 5.19-inch ear hair.

The Sea

Sashimi, Boats, Uncompromising Waters

"The cure for anything is saltwater—sweat, tears, or the sea."
—Isak Dinesen

No, "Isak." From the beach, the sea may *seem* like a cure-all. But once you enter those waters—those deep, rolling waters—the sea is a lot more like a beautiful psychotic woman. She'll woo you, kiss you, and tussle your hair with salt before she starves you, drowns you, and feeds you to the fish. Survival in the depths of the sea is brutal and filthy and short-lived. And on the surface, it's even harder. There are 139 million square miles of open ocean on the planet, each one more unforgiving than the last. But the wide blue is like that beautiful psychotic woman. Who among us can help but pine for her?

THE SEA

PARTS OF A BOAT EVERY MAN SHOULD KNOW

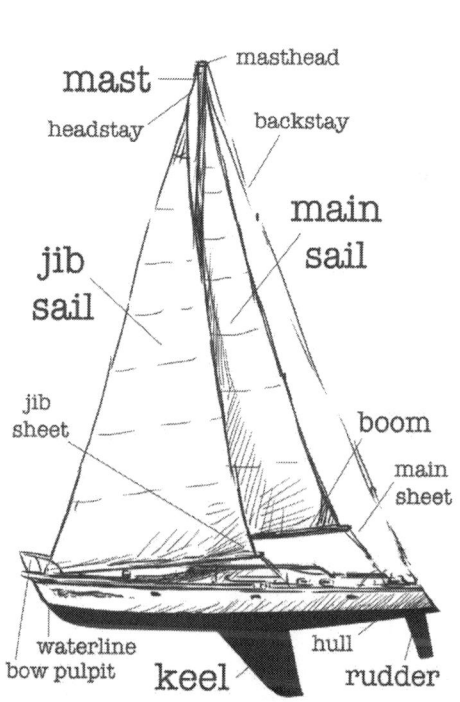

bow (front) - stern (back) - starboard (right) - port (left)

NINE BOATS THAT CHANGED HISTORY

The Raft

Man and beast have used the raft, nature's seagoing vessel of choice, since life first crawled out of the sea. Flat, hull-less, and made of any organic material that floats, rafts became a primary way that life spread across the planet.

After the breakup of the Pangaea supercontinent, biological nonanthropogenic (not man-made) rafts of clumped vegetation enabled flightless animals to populate distant continents and islands.

Until the nineteenth century, man-made rafts were employed primarily as primitive barges, transporting logs downriver. Today they are most commonly used for white-water rafting, an outdoor adventure sport enjoyed by families and drunken teenagers around the world.

The Dugout and the Canoe

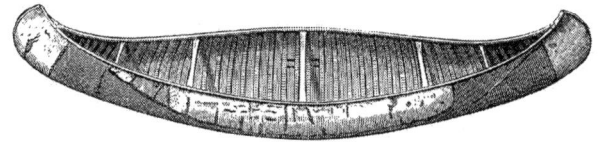

The earliest known engineered water vessels were basic boats made from the hollowed trunk of a single tree. Known as the dugout, logboat, or monoxylon, these simple boats ranged dramatically in size, from single-person vessels to massive army ships, and ancient specimens have been found on nearly every continent. The world's oldest, known as the Pesse canoe, dates all the way back to 8000 BC.

Early northern European models were relatively small and only suitable for tranquil waters. But the Slavs made enormous dugouts, which they sold to the Vikings, who employed the dugouts as the first warships. And halfway around the world, the early Pacific Islanders used giant logboats to begin their epic spread through the world's largest ocean.

While the hulls of the first dugouts rarely strayed from the natural shape of the tree from which they were formed, early boat builders soon discovered the advantages of boats with sharp, pointed edges and formed hulls, leading them to fashion sleek lightweight canoes. Soon wood was scrapped for lighter materials and the canoes evolved to include canvas exteriors built around strong wooden frames.

The canoe is perhaps most commonly associated with Native Americans, who built bark-skinned canoes that were light, durable, and excellent for voyages across rivers, whose shallow waters often necessitated a boat that could be portaged. Northwestern coastal Native American tribes adapted canoes for rivers, lakes, and oceans and for purposes ranging from travel and river fishing to seal and even whale hunting.

When Europeans discovered the Americas, they adapted the canoe for inland exploration. Canoes were utilized by early voyagers such as Alexander Mackenzie, who used a canoe to cross North America in its entirety, and Lewis and Clark, the first Americans to accomplish the same.

The Kayak

The first thing you should know is that "kayak" translates to "man's boat" or "hunter's boat." The second thing you should know is that the early Inuit and Eskimo tribes, who invented the kayak at least 4,000 years ago, were apparently awesome.

The world's first water vessel designed with a covered, watertight deck, known as the skirt or spraydeck, the kayak was a hearty traveling boat. Even the material was impressive: the earliest Inuit kayaks were built with frames of whalebone and skirts made from stretched, stitched sealskin. These watertight skirts allowed the hunters to roll the kayak back upright when it capsized, a necessary innovation considering the Inuit never bothered to learn how to swim (the waters were simply too damn cold for doggie-paddling lessons). In addition, they were hunting huge sea life—seals, whales, and walruses—all of which could knock a kayak end over end.

The Galley

Named for the small sharks that swam the Mediterranean, the galley (from the Middle Greek *galea*) kick-started the future of boat design. Powered primarily by hordes of toiling rowers, the galley was the dugout canoe on steroids, allowing men and materials to travel longer distances and ushering in maritime trade. Virtually all Mediterranean powers quickly adopted the ships, with the Greeks, Romans, Carthaginians, Assyrians, Phoenicians, and Byzantines all using galleys for trade and war.

In its earliest version, the galley could accommodate two sets of fifteen to thirty oarsmen, but a race to develop larger, better galleys for purposes of raiding and warfare led to double-decker banks of rowers on either side. An additional outrigger hull was later added to apply a third bank of manpower.

THE SEA

The largest galleys could accommodate up to 170 rowers in addition to the scores of marines, archers, and even cavalry on the deck above.

The first naval engagement on record, the Battle of the Delta, was fought around 1175 BC between the Egyptians and some group righteously known only as the Sea Peoples. Early galley warfare was limited to pulling up next to one another and attempting to board the other vessel while pelting it with

THE VIKING LONGSHIP

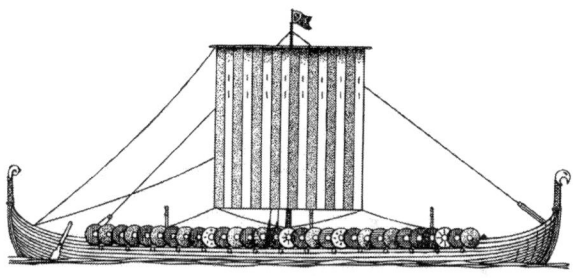

Between the ninth and thirteenth centuries, Vikings used their own versions of the galley, the Viking longship, to raid, trade, pillage, and plunder throughout northern Europe. Like the Mediterranean galley, the Viking longship, was powered by a swarm of rowers. But, unlike their southern contemporaries, the Vikings built their sleek ships so lightweight that the crew could carry them, allowing the marauding Vikings to beach their ships and begin a raid before their unlucky foe had time to prepare.

rocks. But by the eighth century BC, the Greeks had turned the ship itself into a weapon, adding sharp bronze rams beneath the bow's waterline to sink their unsuspecting foes.

In a glimpse of the cannon-driven warfare that would one day dominate the sea, in 672 AD the Byzantine Navy began to attack ships using what became known as Greek fire, an incendiary mixture that would burn on water.

The Sailboat

The sail stands at the top of man's most important innovations. There's only so far we as a species could have gotten with sweat and oars; it was the sailboat that turned the world's oceans and seas into passages for exploration. As early as 3200 BC, the Egyptians and Sumerians had developed square-rigged boats for trading with other civilizations. The ancient Polynesians equipped their double-hulled outriggers with simple cloth sails that helped push their boats from the South Pacific to the islands of Hawaii. The Chinese traveled up and down the Asian continent, trading under sail.

But in the late fifteenth century, sailing boats went from simple means of trade to vessels of global exploration. The change happened with one simple alteration to sail design. While traditional sailboats of the Middle Ages were powered by square-rigged sails that allowed the craft to travel in one direction only, a new style of fore and aft sail design took a couple of the sails and turned them almost 90 degrees. The innovation allowed European ships to sail against the prevailing winds for the first time, freeing captains from the constraints of sailing within known wind patterns. The ocean was about to open up.

By the sixteenth century, the Age of Discovery had become the age of sail. Vast fleets of massive, sail-powered ships took to the sea and any country that wanted to be worth a damn started shipbuilding like crazy. England, Spain, France, Portugal, and Holland suddenly became locked in a race for the globe, vying for control of resource-rich regions in Africa, Australia, Asia, and the New World. And it was the sail-powered ship that enabled the rapid expansion.

The Compass

The Age of Discovery would not have been possible had Europeans not figured out how to pinpoint magnetic north. The compass, the first device capable of determining cardinal directions during cloudy travel days, helped open up the world of navigation. Interestingly, while Europeans probably didn't start making their own compasses until the late twelfth century, the Chinese had been using them since as far back as 206 BC.

THE MANual

The Clipper Ship

The age of sail reached its soaring heights with the advent of the three-masted clipper ship. Introduced at the end of the 1700s, these incredibly fast tall ships became the go-to vessel for speedy trans-ocean crossings. In the Far East, clippers were used to transport lucrative balls of opium throughout Asia and to America and Europe. In the United States, decades before the Panama Canal would revolutionize sea travel, clippers were a primary method of voyaging between New York and gold-rich San Francisco, sailing the length of the two continents, rounding South America's treacherous Cape Horn, and arriving in San Francisco Bay just 100 days later. Even in storms the ships were spectacular. Seasick passengers on slower ships rocked by waves and wind often reported seeing clippers pass them by at full speed as though passing through calm, easy waters.

These majestic ships' glory days were short-lived. In order to achieve their remarkable speeds through narrow hulls, they gave up excessive amounts of cargo space, and when the Suez and Panama Canals opened up and the steam-powered ship came along, their fate was sealed.

The Roaring Forties and Furious Fifties

The fastest way to sail around the globe is to catch a ride on the Roaring Forties, a very strong westerly wind that blows in the Southern Hemisphere just above Antarctica at latitudes ranging roughly from 40 to 50 degrees (thus the name!). The Roaring Forties howl around the globe almost entirely interrupted, allowing sailing vessels to cruise east with remarkable speed.

The most dangerous portion of the journey dips brave captains even farther south into winds known as the Furious Fifties (between 50 and 60 degrees south latitude) as they round Cape Horn. If anyone ever doubted the remarkable capabilities of the clipper ship, this route put the question to rest. It was the favored way for the ships to circumnavigate the globe, taking them from Europe to Africa, Asia, Australia, and back again in as little as seventy-two days. To this day it is known as the Clipper Route.

The Steamer

In 1819 the SS *Savannah*, a hybrid steam and sailing ship, crossed the Atlantic and effectively put an end to the age of sail. The age of the drunken cruise had begun. By 1838 the SS *Great Western* was making scheduled transatlantic journeys between Bristol and New York. A decade later, trading steamers from the California coast were arriving in ports throughout China and Japan.

Though they were unburdened by the fickleness of the wind, nineteenth-century steamboats were no grand solution; they required copious amounts of wood or fuel, leading to pollution and massive deforestation unseen at any other time in history. At one point, so many trees were chopped down along the middle Mississippi that the soil eroded and huge tracts of land flooded.

ONE BIG WRECK

The RMS *Titanic* may be known best for its tragic icy fate, but at the time of its maiden voyage it was known simply as the largest steamship ever built.

THE SEA

Knots

Ever wonder why the speeds of boats are measured in knots rather than miles per hour? The answer lies in actual physical knots. Out of sight of land, sailors could only estimate their speed by casting a rope with evenly spaced knots attached to a piece of wood called a chip log. One sailor would drop the line in the water, letting the knots slip through his fingers while another sailor would time out thirty seconds. The standardized distance between knots (47 feet, three inches) and time (28 seconds), allowed sailors to calculate the ship's speed.

The other main issue was reliability. Early steamboats along the Mississippi were hard to manage and tricky to control; scores were destroyed by collision, fire, or boiler explosions, several of which caused massive losses of life. In 1858, a single boiler explosion on the *Pennsylvania* killed 250 passengers, including Mark Twain's younger brother, Henry Clemens.

Submersibles and Submarines

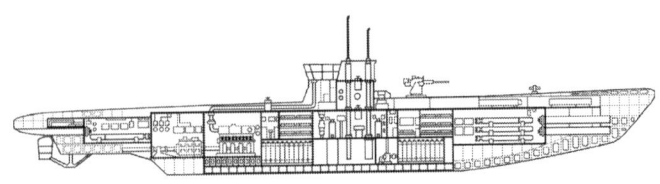

There's one big difference between submersibles and submarines. Submersibles are boats that rely on external help to function underwater; submarines can head out under the waves on their own. But both have been pined over since antiquity. While subaquatic vessels were initially envisioned

Know Your Ship Prefixes

USS: United States Ship
USAV: United States Army Vessel
HMS: His/Her Majesty's Ship (UK)
RMS: Royal Mail Ship/Steamer (UK)
FV: Fishing Vessel
HSC: High Speed Craft
MS: Motor Ship
NS: Nuclear Ship
PS: Paddle Steamer
SS: Steamship (screw-propelled)
SY: Sailing Yacht

as a means of exploring our underwater worlds, the military quickly blew up that romantic notion and nailed the true potential for an undetectable underwater boat.

The *Turtle* got the age of underwater exploration started, albeit very crudely. The rebel Americans used the one-man, hand-powered, acorn-shaped submarine during the Revolutionary War in an unsuccessful attempt to sink a British warship. Despite its unsuccessful attempt at overly complicated sabotage, it was the first boat ever to utilize screw propulsion.

Though both the Union and Confederacy used subs during the Civil War, the technology was not useful until the Russians and Japanese went at it during the Russo-Japanese War. These early U-boats ranged in size from about 67 to 84 feet and could carry fifteen sailors.

Then, during WWI, the Germans began to perfect the art of underwater warfare, using massive fleets of U-Boats to terrorize British and American ships crossing the Atlantic.

Nuclear Ships

In one radioactively charming twist of fate, ship propulsion has come almost full circle to where it began. Where our ancestors 5,000 years ago learned to harness the boundless energy of the wind, we have developed the power to stay at sea indefinitely, without the drawbacks of coal- and diesel-fired engines and without having to rely on the wind. These suckers are nuclear.

In 1954 the United States Navy launched the USS *Nautilus*, the world's first operational nuclear-powered submarine. Today, nuclear reactors power eighty vessels in the Navy's fleet, including submarines, cruisers, destroyers, and huge aircraft carriers. The Nimitz-class aircraft carriers, which sailed all over the world between 1968 and 2006, could stay at sea for an astonishing twenty straight years without refueling. Of course, the bill for these nuclear behemoths is equally staggering—each one cost an estimated $4.5 billion dollars.

Throwing a nuclear power plant on a floating ship might be a little bit dangerous, right? Yes, especially when you consider that in the past half century at least five nuclear-powered subs (three Russian and two American) have been lost at sea. Let's all go scuba diving!

THE SEA

BOSSES OF THE PACIFIC
THE POLYNESIANS

Across the Pacific with a Pig

Around the time Europeans were discovering that there might be a world beyond the Mediterranean Sea, the Polynesians had already spread out across the vastest ocean on the planet. Somehow, in the 64 million square miles of open water in the Pacific, they had found the few specs of islands out there. By 1000 BC, tribes from Taiwan had arrived by boat to the Mariana, Marshall, and Caroline Islands. Within a few centuries they had made it to Tonga and Samoa. From there, the great expansion of the Polynesian societies took off, with large families making perilous voyages south, east, and north, all the way to New Zealand, the remote Easter Island, and Hawaii.

In search of dry land for months on end, the Polynesian navigators brought live pigs, fruits, and vegetables aboard their large, double-hulled canoes. Scores of seafarers died during the journeys, but the venturesome explorers continued to make the voyages for centuries. Researchers believe that Polynesians regularly traveled between Hawaii and Tahiti, despite the 2,700 miles of open ocean separating the island chains, and perhaps even established steady trade routes.

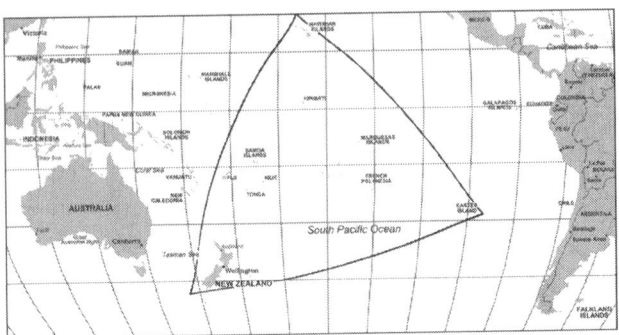

The Polynesian Triangle represents the known areas of exploration and settlement by the ancient Polynesians. In additional to their thriving settlements, the intrepid Polynesian explorers may have even established contact with the inhabitants of South America long before Columbus arrived. Even Antarctica may not have been beyond their reach, as indicated by shards of pottery found on islands just north of the icy continent.

Navigating by the Skin of Their Balls

As every good sailor lost at sea should know, there are plenty of telltale signs of land you can look for (besides actual land). Seagulls, frigates, and other pelagic birds that call land home are a sure sign of dry soil close at hand. In some regions of the world like Tahiti, sailors say you can actually smell the fragrant earth long before you can see the mountains.

But the explorers who first found Hawaii used navigation techniques that make those sight-based methods look like amateur hour at the kiddie pool. While the Tahitian sailors were adept at navigating by the stars, they often used tactical methods to *feel* distant lands. More conservative Tahitian sailors would dip their hands in the water to assess subtle changes in ocean currents as they redirected around islands. The ballsier Tahitians would stand naked at the prow of their boats to detect tiny waves bouncing off land…all with their pendulum-like testicles.

Man Seeks Wooden Raft to Sail Across Pacific

History has had its share of ridiculous theories, but none so outlandish as Thor Heyerdahl's theory of Polynesian origins. A Norwegian student of zoology and geography and an amateur expert in all things tiki, Heyerdahl developed a fierce love of Polynesia and a pretty-far-frickin'-out-there theory that the original inhabitants of the idyllic Tahitian, Easter, and Hawaiian islands were not from Asia but were actually Incan settlers from modern-day Peru. Rather than backing up his theory from a desk in Oslo, Heyerdahl set out to prove it himself.

Heyerdahl moved to Peru and built a 45-foot balsa wood raft he called *Kon-Tiki* using only materials that would have been found in ancient Peru. He then found five other Norsemen insane enough to join him and in 1947 launched *Kon-Tiki* into the Pacific Ocean's swift-moving Humboldt Current.

Not long into the journey, as the crew sailed due west across the largest ocean on the planet, a giant beard of algae and seaweed took root on the underside of the raft. Small fish then showed up, hitching a ride on what was quickly becoming a mobile buffet. With all those tasty little swimmers around, bigger fish joined the party. That, naturally, attracted hundreds of sharks. True to their adventurous nature, the crew of the *Kon-Tiki* invented the sport of open-ocean barehanded shark fishing, which they claimed was "precautionary, should anyone fall overboard."

Miraculously, after just 101 days at sea, *Kon-Tiki* crashed directly into the outer reefs of the Tuamotu Archipelago, breaking up on the sharp reefs. Thor Heyerdahl had proven that it was, after all, possible to sail from Peru to Polynesia way back in the day. Unfortunately, his theory never held up; it was debunked less than a decade later.

IT'S EASIER THAN YOU THINK TO GET LOST AT SEA

Thar She Blows (a Hole in the Side of Your Ship): The Real Moby Dick

Today, Herman Melville's epic sea story, *Moby Dick*, is universally familiar, (even if you haven't read it). Captain Ahab seeks maniacal revenge on the great white sperm whale that lost him his leg. Man is locked in eternal battle with nature. Ahab spots whale, whale sinks ship, and everyone dies save Ishmael, who narrates the tale. Tragic.

Only thing is that old Herman borrowed that story from the true and much, much more horrific saga of the whaleship *Essex*. In 1820, the crew of the 90-foot whaler *Essex* was cruising smack dab in the middle of the vast, 64-million square mile Pacific Ocean, looking to harpoon them some sperm whales and have them a time, when tragedy struck in the form of a giant, torpedo-like sperm whale.

After more than a year of arduous, omen-filled travel, tensions were already high onboard the *Essex* when they spotted their first whale spouts. All hands hit the harpooning boats and left the mother ship behind with a couple sailors to man the controls. Things were going fine until one enormous bull sperm whale, looking as scarred and grizzled as an aquatic Danny Trejo, decided to exact revenge for 5,000 years of whale murder. The bull whale zeroed in on the *Essex* from nearly a quarter mile out and rammed the ship's bow head-on, splintering the hull into toothpicks before disappearing into the depths below. The boat followed shortly thereafter.

The crew looked back at what was left of the *Essex* in horror, immediately realizing they were thousands of miles from salvation with nothing but tiny whaling boats and a couple floating turtles. They salvaged whatever supplies they could and debated their next move. The Marquesas Islands were a mere 1,300 miles upwind, but the sea-wrecked boatmen became convinced that the island was populated by savage cannibals, so they voted to sail east instead. The Marquesas, as sailors around the world soon learned, were inhabited less by cannibals and more by scores of free-loving Polynesian women.

The crew used spare cloth to rig some makeshift sales and chose a rugged, 4,000-mile route all the way back to Chile. With inadequate supplies, twelve of the twenty sailors died along the journey, succumbing to starvation and thirst while surrounded by the largest body of water known to man. And in tragic irony, the eight who survived did so only by eating seven of their deceased comrades. When he was rescued, four months after the *Essex* sank, the captain was found on the floor of his boat, delirious with exhaustion and gnawing on a human bone.

The Momentary Joy of Whaling

A Nantucket sleighride was the exhilarating thrill whalers experienced after harpooning a whale. Attempting to escape its fate, the harpooned whale would drag the whaleboat behind it at speeds up to 25 mph. For many of the whalers, this thrill was likely their last, as their boats were carried over the horizon and lost to the endless ocean.

The Real Robinson Crusoe: Alexander Selkirk

Alexander Selkirk was a grade-A, fist fighting, rabble-rousing a-hole, so naturally he became a pirate. In 1704, at the age of twenty-seven, Selkirk found himself on an English privateering galley named *Cinque Ports* on its way to terrorize Spanish ships off the Pacific coast of South America.

But when the ship rounded Cape Horn and started taking on water, Selkirk freaked out, claiming that the *Cinque Ports* was bound to sink. When the ship reached the remote, barren Juan Fernandez Islands, 370 miles off the coast of Chile, Selkirk could take no more and begged to be left on shore. The captain obliged, dropped off his personal belongings, bid him good luck and sailed north without him. Alexander Selkirk was marooned alone.

Despite the survivalist romance of it, being marooned on a desert island pretty much sucks. It's lonely and, in Selkirk's case, damp and *cold*, with windy, frigid winters dipping into the 30s. But what's worse was that this isolated archipelago had no native animals, which meant any creature accidentally introduced by passing ships thrived. And this meant rats. Thousands of them. Scurrying over the island and devouring anything they could sink their teeth in.

During his first few weeks on the island, the rats attacked Selkirk like he was 150 pounds of prime rib. He stayed as close to the shoreline as possible, hoping in desperation to spot a passing ship, but ended up fleeing inland when scores of hormonal sea lions stormed the beaches to mate.

In the middle of the island Selkirk found the two animal species that would be his salvation: cats and goats. He milked and hunted the feral goats and later sewed himself new rags using their skin. He quickly ingratiated himself to a litter of feral kittens, letting them sleep in his makeshift hut so they could keep the insatiable rats at bay.

Wracked with hunger and loneliness, Selkirk then turned to the goats living on the island for both sustenance and companionship. When he wasn't hunting them, Selkirk would read the bible aloud to the roaming herds of goats. Eventually Selkirk became so adept at goat-catching that when he ran out of ammunition for his only gun, he started running them down and killing the goats by hand.

Despite the less than idyllic life, a Scottish pirate could find himself in worse situations than being marooned on an island. One alternative was being captured by the archenemy Spanish. And on two separate occasions, Spanish ships docked on Selkirk's island, forcing the castaway to play a game of hide-and-go-seek for his life.

Finally, after four years and four months of complete isolation, another British privateering ship named the *Duke* came to his long-awaited rescue. Selkirk quickly repaid the men for rescuing him by employing his new goat-catching skills, feeding the scurvy-ridden sailors their first nutritious meal in months. The captain of the rescue ship was so taken with Selkirk's vitality, ingenuity, and peaceful demeanor that he made him second mate of the *Duke* for the long journey home.

Five Months of Fish and Rainwater

Chinese sailor Poon Lim holds the record for longest survival at sea on a life raft. After the British merchant ship he was sailing on was torpedoed by a German U-Boat in 1942, Lim spent 133 days adrift at sea, the ship's only survivor. After nearly five months alone in the Atlantic, Lim finally made landfall in Brazil.

The Great Wide Pacific: A Record Survival at Sea

In October 2005, five Mexican fishermen set out on what was supposed to be a three-day shark hunt in the Pacific in a 27-foot motorized boat. When they accidentally ran out of fuel, the five men began drifting westward away from the coast of Mexico. Two of the men succumbed to starvation within the first few months, but the other three survivors managed to survive on anything they could find—seagulls, turtles, fish, and shark.

After a record-setting nine and a half months lost at sea, the survivors were spotted by a Taiwanese fishing trawler. When they were rescued, the men were informed they were a mere 200 miles from Australia. They had drifted 5,500 miles, crossing the Pacific Ocean in its entirety.

Frigid Winds and Dogs for Dinner

By the end of the nineteenth century, most of the globe had been "discovered." There was no more sailing to some tropical paradise, dropping anchor, and naming the newfound island and its natives after you. So those men seeking to make a name for themselves turned to the more inhospitable, remote, and uncharted corners of the world. Expeditions set out for the deepest jungles of the Amazon and Congo. Men traversed the dark, cold northern latitudes. And still others headed south to brave the ball-shrinking, freezing hellscape of the last unexplored continent: Antarctica. In just twenty short years between 1897 and 1917, known as the Heroic Age of Antarctic Exploration, seventeen expeditions lost nineteen grizzled men along the way. Those who survived the expeditions returned with remarkable tales and stirring stories of how they managed to escape the frozen wastelands of Antarctica.

One of the most remarkable tales belonged to geologist Douglas Mawson, who led the Australasian Antarctic Expedition of 1911. The expedition, which consisted of thirty men, set out to explore, chart, and bring back specimens from the Great White Continent. After wintering at their base camp near Commonwealth Bay, Mawson split the party into groups, and in 1912 he and two other members, Lieutenant Belgrave Ninnis and skier Xavier Mertz, set out to chart Antarctica's far eastern regions. It was on this journey that his adventure turned into one of the worst nightmares of survival ever documented.

Mawson's Far Eastern Party had made amazing time, traveling over 300 miles from base camp in a month with two teams of sled dogs. Then, on December 14, 1912, seven days before the Southern Hemisphere's summer solstice, disaster struck. One of the expedition's members, Lieutenant Belgrave Ninnis, unwittingly took his sled over a covered crevasse. Thawed by the summer sun and unable to take the weight of the man, sled, and team of huskies, the ground beneath Ninnis opened up and he, the sled, and the dogs vanished into the frozen abyss below. Mawson and Mertz desperately searched in vain for any sign of the lost Ninnis and his sled, which had been carrying their stockpile of food and the party's only tent.

Bereft of the most basic essentials and a third of their party, the two remaining explorers had little chance of surviving the blustery, snow-swept journey that lay ahead. They returned to the previous night's camp and Mawson managed to improvise a tent using some spare canvas and poles by disassembling the remaining sled. With the sled disabled and knowing they would soon run out of food, Mawson began to slaughter the sled dogs for survival, boiling everything from their gamey flesh to their tough feet and livers.

For days Mawson and Mertz struggled on toward base camp, navigating through icy winds that whipped at their weakened frames with relentless force, at times exceeding speeds of 200 miles per hour. Beaten by weather, hunger, and cold, Mertz soon became listless and despondent, insisting on spending a full day doing nothing but recuperating in the relative warmth of his sleeping bag.

Still 100 miles from base camp, Mertz's condition deteriorated further. Periods of lethargic hopelessness were interspersed with violent fits of mania. His skin and hair began to slough off and he was overcome by diarrhea. Mertz died in his sleeping bag on January 8, 1913. Later it was determined that eating the dog's livers probably caused his demise, as dog livers contain *too* much vitamin A and can cause the weakening affliction hypervitaminosis.

After burying his friend, Mawson set off again, when he discovered that the skin on the bottom of his feet was falling off and crippling sores on his soles were soaking his socks with blood. After resting a full day, he continued, only to find himself facing a fate similar to that of Ninnis when he stumbled into a crevasse himself. He would have disappeared into the white depths had his mangled sled not stuck in the ledge. Dangling inside the crevasse, Mawson used all of his remaining strength to haul his body out.

A few days later, and three months after the party had left on their expedition, Mawson finally made it back to base camp. Skinny, weak, and nearly hairless, he arrived just in time to see his expedition's ship disappear over the horizon. Luckily, several of his party had bravely remained behind and Mawson spent the next winter recovering with his friends on the frozen coast of the Antarctic.

Around the World in…Never Mind

In 1968, the UK newspaper *The Sunday Times* hosted a thrilling solo, nonstop sailing race around the world. One of the competitors was an unknown businessman and (very) amateur sailor named Donald Crowhurst. Down on his luck and hell-bent on making a name for himself, Crowhurst ignored the naysayers and launched his ill-equipped boat into the Atlantic on a quest for fame and fortune.

Everything went terribly from the start and, by the time Crowhurst reached the waters off South America, his hopes for making it around the world alive were finished. But would ol' Don give up? Bollocks no! Crowhurst fabricated a complicated logbook and gave untruthful radio reports that showed him on a rip-roaring pace around the globe, and in an era prior to GPS and other location technologies, how the hell was anybody going to prove him wrong? With his web of lies in place, all Crowhurst had to do was wait (completely alone) off the coast of Brazil until the other contestants rounded Cape Horn and passed him on the home stretch. Then, he could simply slip in behind them and finish a respectable, unscrutinized anything-but-first.

Astoundingly, his plan almost worked. That is, right up to the point where the leader of the race abruptly forfeited and the new lead boat suddenly sank. Facing the terrible possibility of winning and having his lie exposed, Crowhurst finally gave up the dream. He cut off his radio and disappeared into the ocean. His ship was found drifting and abandoned but the logbook entries found on board reveal an increasingly tormented mental state. Crowhurst was never seen again.

THE SEA

THERE'S A STORM A BREWIN'
HOW TO TELL THE WEATHER WITHOUT THE DAMN WEATHERMAN

Heading out for a sail? Want to know if you've got a chance to get lost at sea in a storm? You don't need the Weather Channel to know what's coming. The weather is all about pressure. Barometric pressure to be exact. For the sake of simplicity, let's reduce this discussion to two types of pressure: high and low.

High pressure

A high-pressure system means that a bunch of air has been compressed in the upper atmosphere and then descended down to sit somewhere above some godforsaken place like Lubbock, Texas, that hasn't seen rain in a generation. The high-pressure air column is an ornery, solitary piece of sky that forces any weather near it to head in the opposite direction. The predominant winds blow out from the center of the high-pressure system, creating clear skies and, in the summer, hot-as-hell temperatures.

DID YOU KNOW?

Barometric high pressure will cause the bubbles that form at the surface of your coffee to move to the sides of your cup.

Low pressure

Low-pressure systems are, unsurprisingly, just the opposite of high-pressure systems. The air in the upper atmosphere becomes less dense and begins to rise, creating a vacuum underneath. The newly formed vacuum, an insatiably needy bastard, sucks in all the air around it, including cold air from the north and wet air from the south. And what do those two make when they meet up? Storms.

Did You Know?

Because the air in a low-pressure system is less dense than normal, birds have difficulty flying through it, causing them to cruise lower than they normally would. So if you see thousands of birds flying west at breakneck speeds six feet above your head, you might want to batten down the hatches.

Rain's a comin'

On land, the best way to predict rain on your own is through your nose, by sniffing for that earthy, vegetal scent. Before the rainstorm comes, the lower air pressure allows gases in the soil to expand, giving the air an earthy fragrance. The leaves of trees react by opening their stomata, the plant equivalent of pores, to breathe in more carbon dioxide. This planty musk mixes with the earthy fumes to give the sky its rich pre-rain fragrance.

But on the water, things are more difficult to tell. Before the obvious storm clouds approach, you'll be able to spot an oncoming storm by looking at wind direction, cloud type, and wave patterns. In the Northern Hemisphere, weather systems typically move to the east, causing normal westward winds, so a stiff breeze blowing in the opposite direction can indicate a storm on its way. Clouds are a bit trickier. Look for the telltale formation of banded cirrus clouds—wispy, high-forming clouds that string together like cloth—as these indicate an approaching patch of inclement weather.

As the humidity rises ahead of a storm, haze hangs over the sun. True rain experts can observe subtle shifts in wind for insight. A counterclockwise (i.e., north to west) shift means a storm is approaching from the direction the wind is blowing *toward*, as wind moves from high-pressure systems toward areas of stormy low pressure. A clockwise shift in wind (i.e., from north to east or east to south) means good weather is on the way. Why? It's the same thing that makes a hurricane spin.

This Is Why Hurricanes Spin

We can all thank the magical Coriolis effect for the awe-inspiring radar pictures of approaching hurricanes. What is the Coriolis effect? It goes a little something like this: the earth rotates on its axis *fast*. And thanks to the large distance the equator has to travel, the relative speed at the equator is incredible (a blazing 1,038 mph to be exact), whereas at the North Pole, which hardly has any distance to go in a given rotation, the rotation is nice and slow.

This difference in relative rotation speed causes anything, even air, traveling between the pole and equator to curve. Throw a ball hard enough north from the equator and it'll curve westward. Throw that same ball from the North Pole south and it'll curve to the east. Throw a massive amount of air, water, and thunderheads and they'll do the same. As the low-pressure system draws in more and more air from north and south, the curve becomes more pronounced and more visible, eventually forming the characteristic eye and sweeping bands of clouds.

GIANT WAVES

Not only does wind help feed storms and hurricanes, it also creates ocean waves. Whether it's beneath massive storms, or a cloudless, breezy day, wind pressing down on thousands of square miles of ocean begins to generate waves that travel out in all directions across the globe. We normally only come in contact with the waves at the tail end of their journey—on the beach. Though the contact is brief, it can be impressive.

Mavericks, Jaws, Teahupo'o, Ghost Tree, and Cortes Bank are some of the names synonymous with the world's biggest waves. But just why do these waves get so damn big? One word: topography.

The majority of big waves form because of one distinctive feature: an oddly placed seamount. As the wave approaches the shore, the seamount slope causes the wave's center to grow upward and slow down, which bends the faster-moving outer sections of the wave inward toward the building crest. This works to magnify the wave energy at one central peak, turning what would normally have been an impressive 20-foot wave into a monster 80-foot giant.

A Shipper's Nightmare Is a Surfer's Wet Dream: Cortes Bank

When the captain of the steamship *Cortes* spotted a mass of giant, violent waves breaking in the middle of the open ocean, his first thought was that he'd discovered an underwater volcano. It turns out that he'd stumbled upon an uncharted seamount. Located 100 miles west of San Diego, California, Cortes Bank is capped at its highest point by Bishop Rock, which lies just six feet under water. Aside from being capable of producing the astounding 100-foot waves sought after by big-wave surfers around the world, Cortes Bank is one of the Pacific's most treacherous shipping obstacles.

The Largest Wave Ever Surfed (So Far)

In November 2011 Garrett McNamara broke the all-time world record for largest wave ever surfed by riding a 90-foot wave in Nazare, Portugal. To give city-dwellers some perspective, the ride was the equivalent of sliding down the face of a nine-story building.

Rogue Waves

Of all the ocean's impressive phenomena, none have terrified sailors over the centuries as much as rogue waves. The craziest thing about these freak waves is that, until 1995, they were considered by scientists to be as mythical as sea monsters; not one had ever been recorded. That all changed when, on

THE SEA

New Year's Day in 1995, a single 84-foot wave was recorded cruising by the Draupner research platform off the coast of Norway.

But what scientists had, until then, doubted for centuries, seafaring captains had always feared. In one of the most famous accounts, in 1942, the famous steamer RMS *Queen Mary,* loaded with American soldiers headed for England, was broadsided by a rogue wave estimated at 90 feet, forcing the ship to list just a few degrees shy of capsizing.

Rogue waves differ from the monster surfing waves in that they occur in the middle of the open water, where there should be no dramatic shift in wave height. Because these freak waves are so rare, science has yet to get definitive answers on how they form. Most likely they are formed from multiple smaller waves traveling in the same direction that combine energy into one enormous force.

TSUNAMIS

It has been known for centuries in Japan as the village-crushing "harbor wave," called *tsunami* in the native tongue. Hundreds of feet above sea level in the coastal hillside villages of Japan, it's still possible to find ancient rock tablets emblazoned with tsunami warnings, encouraging citizens not to build their homes any closer to the sea. And throughout history, these tsunamis have proven to be the sea's most ferociously destructive force.

Unlike the wind-borne rogue waves that terrorize oceangoing ships or the giant breakers that pound shorelines in Hawaii, California, South Africa, and Portugal, tsunamis are formed from the cold, dark seafloor itself. When the tectonic plates that make up the earth's crust thrust upward or separate, they can displace tremendous amounts of seawater, creating enormous, fast-moving walls of water hundreds of feet tall and a hundred miles wide. Here are five tsunamis that shook the world.

THE SEA

THE WEAPONIZED TSUNAMI

During WWII, Allied forces experimented with creating man-made tsunamis to attack coastal cities and towns of Japan. The idea was to substitute the earth's natural tectonic movement with one huge underwater explosion. Small-scale experiments were carried out with mixed results, but it was too difficult to control the power (and direction) of the killer waves, so the weaponized tsunami was eventually scrapped.

The Original Atlantis: Helike

In the dead of winter in 373 BC, the bustling port city of Helike, Greece, disappeared along with all its inhabitants in the middle of the night. An earthquake in the Mediterranean liquefied the ground underneath the city, dropping it below sea level, and was followed almost immediately by a massive tsunami that left it inundated for all time. For centuries after, visitors to the site claimed that the submerged ruins of the former city could be seen in the waters just offshore. And many scholars believe it was the tragic real-life story of Helike that inspired the story of another city mysteriously lost to the sea: Atlantis.

The Day Portugal Burned and Drowned Simultaneously: The Lisbon Tsunami of 1755

Talk about one-two punches. The 1755 earthquake south of Lisbon was a complete knockout. When the estimated 8.5

magnitude earthquake struck the Atlantic, it shook the Kingdom of Portugal's wealthy capital city for up to five long minutes. Huge scores of elegantly designed stone buildings, built as high as five stories, collapsed, igniting fires that raged around the city.

To escape the growing inferno, many citizens made for the open harbor and crowded onto boats along the waterfront. It was here that they were greeted by a quickly receding sea

THE DEADLIEST OF THE DEADLY: THE 1931 CENTRAL CHINA FLOODS

While hurricanes and typhoons can cause widespread death and destruction, floods have historically been among the world's deadliest natural phenomena. Of these, the 1931 Central China floods took between one and four million lives due to drowning and waterborne diseases, easily topping the charts of the worst disasters in history.

The floods occurred due to a disastrous series of weather events. A two-year drought ended dramatically with a slew of snowstorms and, just as the snow began to melt, China was struck by seven cyclones and prolonged downpours of heavy rain. The flooding destroyed the regions surrounding the Yellow and Yangtze Rivers, some of the most densely populated regions in the world at the time. The catastrophic flooding inundated the valleys with waters 50 feet above normal. Those who didn't die from drowning, cholera, or typhus struggled to survive the economic collapse that followed.

followed by a succession of violent waves ranging in height from 20 feet to over 90 feet that capsized the moored boats and drowned everyone on board. The earthquake and ensuing tsunami killed almost a quarter of Lisbon's 270,000 inhabitants and instilled in the Portuguese king a lifelong fear of living indoors.

The Great Japanese Earthquake of 2011

The tsunami that hit Japan on March 11, 2011, stands as the single most well-documented natural disaster in history. The tsunami, generated by a powerful 9.0 earthquake off the Pacific coast of Japan, overtopped 40-foot defensive tsunami walls, destroying over 400,000 buildings and killing over 15,000 people.

Japan is no stranger to tsunamis; its islands, of course, sit atop the Pacific Ring of Fire in a zone known for megathrust earthquakes. On average, the country is hit by one tsunami every seven years.

The Indian Ocean Tsunami of 2004

The day after Christmas in 2004, a catastrophic undersea earthquake off the Sumatran coast created an 80-foot tsunami that spread out in all directions across the Indian Ocean. The tsunami hit the world's most crowded oceanic coastline, stretching from Africa to India to Indonesia, displacing almost two million coastal inhabitants and killing an estimated 230,000 people.

While the tsunami-prone Pacific Ocean is littered with tsunami tracking buoys, and coastal cities from Tokyo to Honolulu to San Francisco all have tsunami warning systems, until the 2004 tsunami, the coastal population of the Indian Ocean had no early warning system whatsoever. Residents and tourists were still on the beaches when the tsunami hit.

What the Sea Washed In

The power of the 2004 tsunami is still on display in Banda Aceh, Indonesia, where visitors can climb aboard the *Apung 1*, a 2,600-ton ship that broke free of its moorings during the tsunami and was carried nearly two miles inland, coming to rest the middle of the flooded city. The grounds around the wreck have become a touching memorial to the losses suffered on December 26, 2004.

The Sea

MEGATSUNAMIS

Just in case you thought tsunamis were panic-inducing, they've got nothing on their larger, deadlier cousins: megatsunamis. These unearthly waves are created by massive landslides, giant meteors, or the collapse of entire mountains. The power generated creates wave tops that can be as high as 3,000 feet (two Empire State Buildings stacked one on top of the other). Fortunately, they're exceedingly rare. But that doesn't mean they don't happen.

Lituya Bay, Alaska

In 1958, a steep mountainside along the narrow inlet of Lituya Bay, Alaska, suddenly collapsed. The resulting landslide sent an estimated 90 million cubic feet of dirt, trees, and debris splashing down, displacing so much water it created a single wave almost 2,000 feet high. Somehow it killed only five people.

The Looming Disaster: Canary Islands

One of the most worrisome potential sites for disaster is in the Canary Islands off the Atlantic coast of Africa. One particular island in the chain, La Palma, has seen volcanic eruptions on and off for centuries. But after the last large eruption in 1949, the western side of the island actually separated from the eastern side and began slipping into the Atlantic below it.

Although the slide stopped shortly after the volcano did, one trillion tons of volcanic rock currently sits rather precariously above water. If the island collapsed into the water, a megatsunami hundreds of feet high would wash across the Atlantic, devastating the East Coast of the United States from Miami to New York. The good news? Scientists predict the event will most likely happen, but not for another 10,000 years.

THE SEA'S MOST DANGEROUS ANIMALS

Puffer Fish: Get High or Die Trying

The first sign you've ingested a fatal dose of puffer fish, the world's second deadliest vertebrate, is when your lips go numb. Then, after throwing up for a bit, it's your whole body's turn. Finally, in addition to the onset of paralysis, your heart rate skyrockets, your blood pressure plummets, your lungs stop working, and then you slip painfully into a coma and probably die.

Yet, despite the possibility of incurable death, the toxic puffer fish is a highly sought-after delicacy in Japan, Korea, and China, where experienced chefs prepare tasty meals ranging from puffer fish sashimi to puffer fish soup. If the chef uses *just* the right amount of poisonous meat, the patron will

> ### A Recipe for Zombieism
> Sushi chefs aren't the only ones who prepare meals using puffer fish. There is ample evidence that Haitian witch doctors once fed their victims a mixture containing several toxins, including the puffer's tetrodotoxin, causing the consumer to enter a death-like trance and become what is known in Creole as a *zonbi*.

become pleasantly intoxicated, but a bit too much of the fish's toxin and it's the diner's last supper.

Box Jellyfish: The Invisible Killer

These notorious little box jellyfish, found in the waters near Australia, are impressive killers. The "sea wasps," as they're kindly called, have hundreds of thousands of miniature venom-injecting javelins in each of their tentacles, capable of killing a full-grown man in as little as five minutes. The danger the box jellyfish poses to humans is compounded by its near invisibility. The jellyfish is translucent and, unfortunately, tends to hang out near beaches. Although it is rarely deadly if treated quickly, jellyfish stings kill around thirty people per year in the Philippines alone, where the antivenin is rare.

Stonefish: Camouflaged Agony

As its name implies, the stonefish looks a whole lot like a rock or coral, making it dangerously difficult to spot and easy to step on. Unlike other fish that just swim away, these jerks stay still and raise their spike-lined dorsal fin like a mohawk, injecting its oh-so-deadly venom into any bumbling surfer who wades too close. The pain of a stonefish sting is so horrifically unbearably that victims regularly beg to have the afflicted region amputated.

The Red Sea Fire Urchin: The A-Hole

The only thing worse than getting stung by the deadly Red Sea Fire Urchin is getting stung *and* bit by the deadly Red

Sea Fire Urchin. If this colorful urchin fails to kill you by piercing you with its venomous shell, it also has the ability to inject your foot with venom from its anus-like mouth. That's just messed up.

Sea Snake: The Moody Murderer

Sea snakes like to hang out in warm, tropical waters and are among the most venomous snakes in the world. Fortunately, they tend to be kind and forgiving of humans and often hold back a bit when they bite, releasing only trace amounts of venom. However, if the snake is in a particularly bad mood when it bites, its victim will go through a miserable series of symptoms, beginning with sweating, headache, and nausea, progressing to a terrible full-body ache, and ending with paralysis, respiratory failure, muscle breakdown, dark reddish-brown urine, and ultimately cardiac arrest.

Stingray: The Scuba Slayer

Any fish deadly enough to kill a man no croc could do in deserves some respect. The stingray, a fish related to sharks, has a tail lined with highly venomous stingers, which it uses exclusively for protection. The fish will whip its stinger into the perceived threat—often leaving the venom-laden spine *in* the victim's wound. A stingray sting rarely causes death, but can be fatal if the sting slices open an artery or occurs near a vital organ.

Blue-Ringed Octopus: Murder by Kisses

The blue-ringed octopus's bite is so soft its victims often don't know they've been bitten until they find themselves unable to breath or move. The venom of this octopus is a cocktail of deadly neurotoxin chemicals similar to that in the puffer fish. Death feels the same too: victims are fully aware of the fact that they've been rendered totally helpless and are unable to move or cry for help. If the bitten victim doesn't receive artificial respiration quickly, there's a darn good chance that they'll suffocate to death.

Killer Whale: The Sadistic Pack Hunter

Although we almost excluded killer whales from this compendium of seaborne death-harbingers because they aren't inherently dangerous to humans AND because of their back-asswards matrilineal social system (pods of killer whales are led by females), we ultimately felt obliged to include them because they engage some of the most gloriously badass hunting techniques anywhere on earth. They definitely deserve to have "killer" in their name.

Hunting alone, the 30-foot killer whales use their superior size and strength to kill or immobilize prey, such as large fish, seals, sea lions, and even smaller sharks, by either whipping them with their powerful tails or by ramming them at full speed with their giant noggins. These head butts can be particularly gruesome, as a well-located orca ram can cause a prey's internal organs to explode upon contact.

But when hunting for larger prey in groups, killer whales get all strategical. They'll take out dolphins, sharks, mink whales, grey whales, and, on occasion, the blue whale (the largest animal to ever exist). Hunting these giants takes incredible patience and cooperation, which has earned the killer whales the title "wolves of the sea." Groups will target a weak-looking prey and, after successfully separating the weakling from its group, take their time to kill it. Instead of attacking their prey, they drown it, either by enclosing it from above to prevent surfacing or by physically holding it underwater—sometimes upside down—until it suffocates.

Saltwater Crocodile: The True Man Eater

What's a crocodile doing at sea? It's crushing your bones in the warm, salty sand. It's also the only true man hunter on this list and holy crap is it terrifying. Saltwater crocodiles are massive and, when they get hungry, they'll feed on anything. That includes birds, monkeys, kangaroos, wild boar, water buffalo, tigers, lions, sharks, and humans.

In addition to their size (up to 20 feet long and 2,000 pounds), saltwater crocodiles are quick, immensely strong, and highly territorial, treating intrusive humans—on land or even in boats—like an enemy worth tasting. While no reliable data exists, experts estimate that saltwater crocodiles fatally attack around fifteen people per year.

> ### THE BATTLE OF RAMREE ISLAND
> During WWII, the Allied forces drove about 1,000 Japanese soldiers into the murky, crocodile-infested swamps of Ramree Island, off the coast of Burma, trapping the soldiers in the waters. As many as 400 Japanese soldiers may have been killed by saltwater crocs.

Great White Shark: Yeah, Just Plain Terrifying

Great whites are infamous killers, suspected each year of attacking swimmers, surfers, and boaters with their powerful jaws and razor-sharp teeth. These predatory fish are *huge*, reaching lengths of up to 20 feet and weights exceeding 4,000 pounds. The good news for swimmers and surfers is that these sharks enjoy meals high in fat, like seals, sea lions, dolphins, tuna, whales, and, you know, other sharks.

Unfortunately, great whites don't know exactly how scrawny you are, so they tend to take *test bites*, after which the shark might determine that you would, in fact, be a pretty awful meal. But a shark's nibble is a bit more powerful than need be—it can sever your arm, leg, or torso. Of the 129 victims of shark attacks in the last twenty-five years, at least twenty-nine have bled to death.

SOME RELIEVING FACTS ABOUT SHARK ATTACKS

You Have a Better Chance of Being Killed by a Bee

There are a lot of things statistically more dangerous than sharks: freak fireworks accidents, being struck by lightning inside your house, undercooked sausage attack, walking down the street. So, really, don't worry about it.

There Aren't Many Great Whites in the World

Taking a dip in the ocean? Worried you may immediately be eaten by a great white à la *Jaws*? Fear not: great whites are considered an endangered species with a worldwide population estimate of just a few thousand. You should feel free to go in past your ankles.

Just Stop Peeing

Sure, it's one of the greatest feelings in the world. The cool ocean enveloping your body, the warm urine dissipating all around you. You're adding your own salty water to the ocean. But do you know what else pees in the ocean? Dying seals. And do you know what loves dying seals? Sharks.

You Can Fend Off a Shark

If you do happen to find yourself mid–shark attack, it is possible to fend off the fish. Experts suggest punching, poking, or grabbing at the eyes and gills—pretty much the only sensitive areas on the sharp-toothed fish.

THE SEA

WHAT'S IN MY SUSHI?

Real men love sushi, and that is not a euphemism. The Japanese delicacies of *sashimi* and *nare-zushi* (sushi) offer everyday landlubbers an authentic taste of the sea. And chances are you, my friend, are a landlubber. So, before you take to the open ocean or your local sushi bar, let's learn you something about the creatures of the sea/delicious rolls on your plate.

The Two Most Popular Rolls

Tuna rolls (Maguro/Tekka)

Aside from sharks, *Thunnus* are the most ubiquitous apex predators in the world's oceans. These behemoths of the deep can grow up to 15 feet long and 1,000 pounds. In addition to their staggering size, tunas use massive, oxygen-rich muscles to reach speeds nearing 50 miles per hour while hunting. Unfortunately, overfishing has severely depleted the numbers of fish worldwide, resulting in some insane prices for sashimi. Currently, the record amount of money paid for a single, 600-pound tuna is over $730,000 at Tokyo's Tsukiji Fish Market.

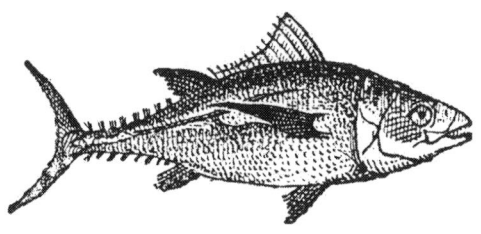

California rolls

Even the poor saps among us that failed to develop a taste for raw fish can usually enjoy a California roll or two. The essence of Americanized sushi, the California roll consists of rice (on the outside), seaweed, avocado, cucumber, *tobiko* (flying fish roe) or sesame seeds, and imitation crabmeat. What is imitation crabmeat, you ask? It's much more complicated than you think.

This oddly flavorless, shapeless seafood filling is actually a hugely popular product in Japan called *kamaboko*, which is made from pulverized white fish meat (usually haddock or pollack) that is minced to a fine white paste and mixed with a bunch of random ingredients, like MSG and egg whites, to give it that "authentic" crustacean texture. Add a layer of red food coloring and voilà, you've got some authentic, grade-A *krab* meat.

Melanogrammus aeglefinus, *or the common crab-wannabe.*

MASCULANEOUS

THE MAGIC OF KELP

Don't care for seaweed? You might like it more than you know. Carrageenan, a compound found in red kelp, is used as a thickening agent in everyday products, including toothpaste, shampoo, sunscreen, peanut butter, ice cream, soy milk, processed ham, and even beer.

A Japanese Sushi Menu (Before It Hits Your Plate)

Squid (Ika)
The "giant" version of these cephalopods can grow up to 45 feet long.

Puffer fish (Fugu)
Very little of this Japanese delicacy is edible; the rest of it carries a powerful neurotoxin called tetrodotoxin.

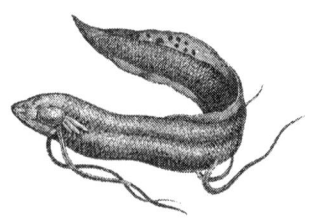

Eel (Unagi/Anago)
Consider the Japanese eel a salmon in reverse: it leaves its freshwater home to spawn hundreds of miles away in the middle of the ocean.

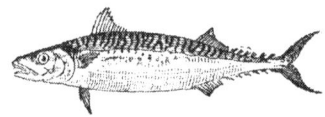

Mackerel (Saba)
Mackerel, macrill, mackarell, macquerel, mackril, not only does the name "mackerel" stand for dozens of different small coastal fish, there have been at least nineteen different ways of spelling it.

MASCULANEOUS

Salmon (Sake)

After traveling through the ocean their whole adolescent lives, salmon always manage to make a beeline for the same river they were born in when it's time to mate.

Flying fish roe (Tobiko)

You're probably used to this fish's delicious eggs, but the non-embryonic adult version can "fly" out of the water for up to 650 feet while getting 19 feet above the surface of the sea.

Octopus (Tako)

Octopuses are so intelligent that experts theorize they have a level of problem-solving skills similar to that of a three-year-old human child.

Sea urchin (Uni)

The spiny, hedgehog-like sea urchin is actually a close relation to the sand dollar. The gonads and roe are the most popular edible parts.

Masculaneous

Heroes, Villains, Adventure, and Intrigue

THE FASCINATINGLY DISHONEST ORIGINS OF EVERYDAY PLACES

Everything has its own intriguing story of creation. Plastic was invented as a substitute for ivory billiard balls and New York City was founded as a fur trading post. Some innovations come about from moments of human genius, others from the tragedy of war or by total accident. But some are the intentional or inadvertent creations of the more dishonorable peoples of the world: the thieves, brigands, drug dealers, and unsavory characters who have, in their own weird way, shaped history. Here are a couple of their stories.

How the Highwaymen Lit Up London

By the seventeenth century, London was among the world's largest cities. But with just 225,000 citizens in 1605, it resembled more a large town than a thriving metropolis. In fact, the areas immediately surrounding the city were still wooded countryside where unlit dirt roads wound from the country's capital to towns like Bath, Exeter, and Dover. It was on these roads that a new form of criminal was born: the highway robber. Highwaymen, as they were called, would set up shop on isolated, well-covered stretches of road, lying in wait for unprotected stagecoaches carrying wealthy travelers. Though they were armed with pistols, they were ever the gentlemen, avoiding violence whenever possible by making a dashing escape on horseback.

Their exploits quickly reached folk-hero status in the eyes of England's impoverished masses, who dubbed them "the Gentlemen of the Road," either because they robbed only the rich or because they employed an eccentric, gentlemanly flare while doing it. Each one was a character. Captain James Hind, for example, refused to rob anybody but the wealthy members of England's parliament. The well-dressed Claude Duvall was exceedingly polite to the people he held up.

Highway robbery became so fashionable that it even spilled into London proper. During 1690, robberies were so com-

A COLORFUL EXECUTION: THE HANGING OF JOHN "SIXTEEN STRING JACK" RANN

One of the most famous highwaymen was John "Sixteen String Jack" Rann, a thief whose wit and flamboyant robbing attire made him an extremely popular figure. While on the job, Rann always wore wild outfits, such as breeches decorated with sixteen colorful silk strings. He once showed up to his own trial wearing flowers in his suit and bright blue ribbons cascading from his iron shackles. Even at his own execution, in 1774, the twenty-four-year-old Rann maintained his charming, happy-go-lucky demeanor. Wearing a lovely, newly tailored pea-green suit, he bantered playfully with the crowd, joked with the executioner, and performed a little jig before he was hanged.

mon in Hyde Park, the city's largest public commons, that King William III was forced to commission the construction of Rotten Row, a wide road passing through the southern stretch of the park illuminated by over 300 oil lamps, the first streetlights in London.

The Island Bought with Opium

A Chinese opium den circa 1860.

If you think our current trade deficit with China is bad, it's nothing compared to what Britain faced back in the late 1600s. Four hundred years ago, just about everything European citizens wanted was made in China. Tea, porcelain, silk: The land was like one bourgeois warehouse and people from Italy to Britain couldn't get enough.

Before long, Britain's state-sponsored corporation in the region, the British East India Company, was creeping in on the action. British merchant ships landed in the Chinese ports of Macau and Guangzhou eager to fill their holds with all the exotic valuables they could without capsizing.

Problem was, there wasn't much the Chinese wanted from the Europeans. A primarily agrarian culture, the Chinese were proudly self-sufficient and looked down upon most of the European-made goods the merchant ships were trying to barter. Who could blame them? Nobody wants Scottish wool underpants when they could get a cheaper version in silk.

Pretty much the only thing the Chinese would take for their tea, cloth, and plate ware was silver. And, surprise surprise, silver was expensive. Pretty soon the British ran out of the metal entirely and had to start buying it from other European powers just so they could shuttle it off to China. The British government wasn't having it.

So what did the British do? What any slightly evil empire would: They organized a massive, state-sponsored drug cartel, run by none other than the world-famous East India Company. What the British Empire lacked in sensual underwear they more than made up for in opium. Two of their colonies, India and Bengal, were chock-full of poppy fields. The Chinese people had no idea what was in store for them.

By the time the eighteenth century rolled around, thousands of Chinese villagers were partying on copious amounts of

opium like it was, well, 1699. Impressive quantities of the drug, rolled up into enormous, sticky poppy balls, were entering the Chinese ports and you could hardly find a single merchant that remembered what silver looked like.

What's really astounding is that Britain's drug pushing in China doesn't just subsist for a couple decades; it goes on for hundreds of years, right up to the Communist Revolution. But way back at the time that the Chinese Qing Empire began earnestly cracking down on opium use, the damage had been done. Thousands upon thousands of Chinese were full-blown addicts and opium was flowing in through the country's border like it was a sieve.

Finally, the Chinese government came down hard on the Anglo dealers. They closed rivers to commercial trading, raided ports, confiscated 11,000 pounds of opium, and made 1,600 arrests. The sweeping drug bust in China was massive. (To put it in perspective, the Drug Enforcement Agency's famous 1991 heroin bust, the largest of all time, netted just 1,000 pounds of heroin with a street value of around $4 billion.)

And what did the Chinese get for it? A big, fat war. Two of them actually. Being cut off from their lucrative customer base royally pissed off the British government and they retaliated in 1839 by sending in Her Majesty's Royal Navy. By 1843, everything had fallen apart for China. The British had taken control of the mouth of the Yangtze River, laid siege to Guangzhou, and decimated China's Navy.

The Chinese sued for peace. And in return the British were granted Treaty Ports in what became Canton, Shanghai, and Fuzhou. But one of the biggest concessions came when the Chinese government officially ceded control of the island of Hong Kong to the British government. The island that opium bought was finally returned to the Chinese government in 1997.

Hoover's Sin City

For all its modern debauchery and notorious reputation, Las Vegas, Nevada, was left out of the Wild West completely. Billy the Kid, the O.K. Corral, the Lincoln County War, Wyatt Earp: They were all elsewhere. When a small fort finally sprang up in Vegas, it was abandoned. The Mormons moved in for a while…and then left. For over a century Las Vegas remained a dusty outpost, a stop on a route to a better place. Even right up to 1930, as Americans flooded west, Las Vegas only managed to attract a couple thousand residents.

That all changed with a river and one of the most ambitious engineering projects in US history: the Hoover Dam. At the start of the 1930s, with the country in the throes of the Great Depression, new forms of employment were desperately needed. The United States, recently electrified, was also starting to demand electricity. The Colorado River could provide both. Desperate to do something to help get the nation on the right track, President Herbert Hoover agreed to the construction of a massive damn across the river's Black Canyon.

As soon as construction started, Las Vegas ballooned four-fold in population with tens of thousands of down-on-their-luck, unattached men wandering into the dusty outpost, hoping for work at the dam. Now, where there are tens of thousands of single men, there are needs. By 1931, with the dam still five years from completion, the first gambling license had been issued to the Northern Club (the current site of La Bayou Casino) and later that year The New Frontier Hotel and Casino broke ground on what would eventually become the world-famous Las Vegas Strip. All thanks to a president's dam.

THE ORIGINAL SIN CITY

In the 1850s, when Las Vegas was still a dusty outpost, it was New York City that owned the title City of Sin. On the island of Manhattan alone, there were hundreds of saloons, opium parlors, and gambling halls, and over 30,000 prostitutes working at any given time, one for every sixty-six people living in the city.

Cocaine City

> *"I'm a decent man who exports flowers."*
> —Pablo Escobar

Yes, and Miami was built with sweat, orange juice, and honest hard work. In the 1960s, Miami was about as far from its current incarnation as a glamorous metropolis as it could have been. The city of just 250,000 people was sleepy and quiet, with a shadow of a downtown, citrus groves throughout the suburbs, and family-friendly resorts dotting the beaches. All that was going to change thanks to a white powder from South America.

The Florida peninsula, the continental United States' southernmost point, juts into the Atlantic and Caribbean like one large, inviting landing strip. And during the 1970s and 1980s, that was exactly how it was used. In the early 1970s, cocaine, previously a scarce drug in the United States, began to trickle in from South America. Then, in 1975, an enterprising gangster named Pablo Escobar took control of the cocaine trade in Medellín, Colombia, and the spigots into the United States opened.

Escobar picked Miami as the top destination for his drug shipments. The wide-open seaports, rural suburbs, and proximity to the Caribbean Islands and South and Central America made it the easiest place to bring drugs into the country. The shipments, which soon topped out around half a billion dollars each day, required a brand-new cottage industry in America. Thousands of people were employed to transport, store, and move the cocaine from Miami to the rest of the country. The industry generated billions of untaxed, dirty dollars that needed to be spent somewhere. What better place than a tropical paradise?

Before the Federal Government had fully wised to the extent of the cocaine trade, the entire economy of the city of Miami was skyrocketing thanks to it. The previously subdued downtown grew upward with dozens of skyscrapers financed in cash. High-end stores moved into previously vacant lots all over the city. And within twenty years, Miami had nearly doubled in size.

Today, the city's sordid past has largely been forgotten. Instead, its glittering downtown, glamorous beach resorts, and seaside boutiques have turned Miami into one of the nation's top tourist destinations. But it was all made possible by a little criminal ingenuity and a whole lot of coke.

The Brief Life of Pablo Escobar

Pablo Escobar's life is a rags-to-riches story, where the riches are billions of dollar bills, each of which contains trace amounts of cocaine.

As a young boy, Pablo Escobar set himself the lofty goal of becoming a millionaire before his twenty-second birthday. He started by trying every criminal enterprise he could, dabbling in selling fake lotto tickets and stolen cigarettes, auto theft, and kidnapping. Eventually Escobar landed on one lucrative business: drug trafficking.

With a single plane, Escobar began transporting cocaine through Panama and into the United States. By the 1980s, Escobar was the king of cocaine, controlling an estimated 80 percent of the world's entire freaking market. Daily flights were moving an astounding estimated 15 tons of coke across the US border, earning Escobar a net worth between three and thirty billion dollars. Based on those figures alone, if he

were alive today, he would be the seventh richest person in the world.

Escobar's drug-fueled rise to the top was short-lived. In 1991 he was arrested and imprisoned in a Colombian jail called La Catedral, widely referred to as Hotel Escobar. Like all good criminals with an eye on the future, Escobar had helped design the prison himself. Hotel Escobar was less of a prison and more of a, well, hotel; it was equipped with a soccer field, a bar, a Jacuzzi, a decorative waterfall, and, for some reason, an oversized dollhouse.

How the Fall of a Kingdom Gave Birth to the Mafia

Sicily has always been a troubled island. It's wracked with oppressive heat blowing off of Africa and it has volcanoes, tsunamis, and earthquakes. But more than anything, its strategic position, smack dab in the middle of the most fought-over sea, has gotten it nothing but trouble, politically. In little more than 2,700 years since the Greeks first founded the southern city of Syracuse, the island of Sicily has changed hands to no fewer than eight foreign powers, ranging from the Romans, Vandals, and Arabs to the Normans, Swabians, and Spanish.

So it was no wonder that, when Italy finally annexed the island kingdom in 1860, they found that the Sicilian citizens wanted very little to do with their brand new stable government. And no sooner had the yoke of feudalism been thrown off than the first taste of the mafia had begun. After the dissolution of the feudal kingdom, with little government protection from mainland Italy and virtually no police, scores of desperate peasants had turned to petty banditry to survive and were swarming through the farms of western Sicily.

For the farm owners, the *mafiosi*, a butchering of the Arabic word for "bravado," was the answer. The newly minted landowners, most of them former peasants, began hiring whatever able-bodied men they could, many of them former thieves and violent bandits themselves, to protect their valuable citrus orchards from outside criminals. Now, if it sounds like a potentially bad idea to have criminals hired to go after criminals, it was. More often than not, the newly formed patrols began colluding with the thieves on the other side and before long each town's independent militia had become its own little crime organization.

By the waning years of the 1800s, the Mafia was fully entrenched in Sicily. The small village bands had coalesced into larger crime syndicates. Eight separate clans (*cosche*) operated in the suburbs around Palermo alone. They bought politicians, planned kidnappings, forged money, and murdered witnesses. Elaborate initiation ceremonies created lifelong members in what they called *cosa nostra* ("our thing"). And in return for a lifelong commitment, any member sent to jail had both his family and his legal fees taken care of.

GANGSTER WITH A HEART OF GOLD

Alphonse Gabriel Capone, America's most famous mobster, amassed an incredible $100 million fortune (worth over $1 billion today) from bootlegging liquor during Prohibition. Capone was vilified for his powerful criminal organization as well as his excessive acts of violence like the Saint Valentine's Day Massacre. Yet Capone always stayed true to his Sicilian Mafia roots; like the earliest members of the Mafia, he made sure he took care of his own. As his gang's prominence grew, Capone paid for daily milk to be delivered to Chicago's schoolchildren and opened soup kitchens to help combat the pain of the Depression among the area's Italian immigrants.

 THE MANual

AWESOME ADVENTURES THAT WERE PROBABLY A TERRIBLE IDEA

Neil Armstrong's Life Insurance

On July 16, 1969, Apollo 11 lifted off from the Kennedy Space Center in Florida and headed toward the moon. Four days later, after traveling 238,900 miles, Neil Armstrong, Buzz Aldrin, and Michael Collins touched down on the lunar surface. The grainy black-and-white shots beamed back to the rest of us earthlings were amazing. But while America celebrated a great triumph, all of NASA was secretly holding their breath. That's because voyaging to the moon during the 1960s was about the most dangerous thing you could do.

Before the Apollo 11 moon landing, NASA had sent kamikaze crafts to practice. Each one of the Ranger spacecrafts crashed spectacularly into the surface of the moon while relaying thousands of images of the lunar surface back to Earth. The first mission, Ranger 4, just seven years before Armstrong's first steps, managed to send back a whopping zero images before its demise. Considering the plan was to land a man on the moon within the decade, things were not off to a good start.

If that wasn't enough to make the astronauts nervous, there was more. When the healthy, athletic thirty-eight-year-old

Neil Armstrong tried to acquire life insurance before his flight, the estimated annual dues came in at roughly three times his yearly salary. Not one to give up on mankind, Armstrong and the rest of the crew took matters into their own hands and went about ensuring their families' future comfort by signing hundreds of photographs that were to be sold should Apollo 11's voyage turn into a one-way trip.

The Accidental Invention of the Road Trip

In 1903, fifty-three long years before the Interstate Highway System was even conceived, Horatio Nelson Jackson invented the cross-country road trip. On a stopover in San Francisco, California, Jackson was talked into a $50 bet that said ain't nobody could drive an automobile from the Pacific Ocean to the Atlantic. Despite being a crappy driver, Jackson took the bet, bought himself a brand new (whopping) twenty-horsepower Winton, enlisted a twenty-two-year-old mechanic as a driving partner, and set out to drive across the continent.

Understandably, things went terribly. In 1903 the western United States was still, well, the Wild West. Most dusty towns they passed had never seen a paved road, let alone an *auto-mo-bile*. At times, the Winton, which Jackson named the *Vermont*, broke down every few miles, blowing tires like they were party balloons. Finally, sixty-three days after leaving San Francisco, the *Vermont* sputtered into New York City, becoming the first automobile to drive from sea to shining sea. As for the $50 bet, Jackson never managed to collect it.

 THE MANual

From Cape Town to Cairo, All for a Fine Piece of Tail

How far will a man go for a fine woman? In 1898, British adventurer Ewart Grogan took the question literally and answered: 6,000 miles. In an effort to convince his crush's wealthy stepfather that he was worthy of his stepdaughter's hand in marriage, Grogan walked nearly 6,000 miles from Cape Town, South Africa, to Cairo, Egypt. During the trek he was stalked by lions and headhunters and had a number of his party die from malaria. But, by the time he arrived in Cairo, he'd managed to win the woman's hand and became a folk hero for being the first European to walk the length of the African Continent.

How Smallpox Misplaced a City

When the first Spanish and Portuguese explorers arrived in South America and ventured into the dense jungles of the Amazon, they came across the incredible ruins of an abandoned city. They took detailed notes about grand archways, planned-out city streets, and neatly rowed gardens. The only thing they couldn't record, in the middle of the vast forest, was the location of the mysterious city. And for the next 175 years, men tried in vain to find it.

One of those men was Percy Fawcett. In 1925 the former British officer and experienced adventurer was fifty-seven years old. He had fought in the trenches of WWI, climbed mountains, and led some of the most extraordinary expeditions of discovery through Peru and the most remote sections of the Brazilian Amazon, disappearing into the forbidding jungle only to return years later, healthy, unscathed, and leading his brutally depleted parties.

But despite his lifetime of success and bravery, one thing consumed Fawcett: what he called the Lost City of Z. It was those first reports from the Conquistador explorers that gripped his interest. The idea that there was once a thriving city somewhere in the richest, most uninhabitable jungle on earth was enough to drive him mad.

And so, on April 20, 1925, Fawcett led his small expedition party, including his own son, into the heart of the Amazon rainforest near the Xingu River and only a couple dozen miles from the most remote place on earth.

Neither he nor anyone from his party was ever heard from again.

Most people assumed he had been killed by the uncontacted tribes of the upper Xingu River. Others thought he had simply been lost in the jungle.

What's incredible is that not only were the original stories of the "lost city" true, but that Fawcett was possibly standing on top of it as he made his way up the Xingu. In 2008, an anthropologist from the University of Florida uncovered a massive settlement covering nearly 8,000 square miles at the headwaters of the Xingu River. The area was once home to as many as 50,000 inhabitants living in twenty-eight separate "towns," each with an enormous wooden plaza at the center. From the town plazas, long, maintained roads stretched out, some lined with carved canals for trade via canoe.

For more than a thousand years, the people of this vast Amazonian civilization flourished. But when the first Europeans landed in South America, the diseases they brought with them, like smallpox, traveled faster than they could. Frightened, diseased citizens wandered from town to town in search of help and the illnesses spread throughout the entire Amazon so quickly that, by the time the Spanish caught up with the diseases they'd brought, there was nobody left.

Unfortunately for Percy Fawcett and the explorers that followed him into the Amazon in the decades to come, there was no physical city packed with riches to find. The inhabitants of the so-called lost city built their thriving metropolis with wood instead of stone. By the time Fawcett reached the Xingu, the voracious jungle had swallowed up every last sign of its former inhabitants. All that was left were subtle outlines of the city in the landscape and a rich history of culture buried just beneath the soil.

FIVE SUPERHUMAN POWERS NOW WITHIN YOUR GRASP

We thought we would end *The MANual* with a brief look toward the future. Here are a few exciting innovations that may one day revolutionize your life.

Mr. Insomniac

For centuries, common man has been encumbered by one crippling, time-sucking daily need: sleep. And countless souls have strived to limit its incessant necessity. Thomas Edison, Winston Churchill, and Nikola Tesla all lived by a polyphasic sleep schedule that broke daily sleeping into two or more brief catnaps, adding up to a total of about three hours of sleep per day.

THE MANual

Finally, all that sleep scheduling became obsolete at the dawn of the twenty-first century with a magical drug called Modafinil. Originally designed to keep narcoleptics from randomly falling asleep mid-sentence, the true genius of the drug was soon brought to light (by who other than the US military?). On Modafinil, you can stay awake forever. And unlike with caffeine, cocaine, or methamphetamines, the wakefulness you feel on this magical pill is as steady and normal as though you just woke up.

Of course, what's a superpower without a crippling side effect? Modafinil's Kryptonite turns out to be its tendency to cause toxic epidermal necrolysis, a disorder in which the top layer of your skin sheds off like a snake's. Except, instead of emerging from your layer of dead, old skin even more awesome and powerful, in the case of Modafinil, you just have a very good chance of giving in to that proverbial eternal sleep.

The Incredible Ant

For decades scientists have pursued a miracle: building an Iron Man–like mechanical exoskeleton suit that would allow people with crippling disabilities like paralysis to walk again. And for decades it seemed a pipe dream of the future.

Welcome to the future. Well, almost. As quickly as the human race adopted smartphones, we may also soon be using helpful exoskeletons in our day-to-day lives. Beyond full-body contraptions to give the disabled the power to walk again, the US military's current project is called the Human Universal Load

Carrier (HULC). A lightweight support system that attaches to the legs, feet, and back, the hydraulic system would help soldiers in the field carry packs up to 200 pounds for hours with the same effort they'd use to carry a fanny pack.

The suit technology has advanced so quickly that components that weighed hundreds of pounds less than a decade ago now come in at a total of just 30 pounds. The only huge hurdle still facing the quest to become a real life Iron Man is, of course, energy. Using a full-body exoskeleton to move hundreds of pounds of gear takes a lot of power and so far there haven't been small batteries capable of the task. One early prototype even failed because it had to be plugged into the wall to be used.

Okay, so maybe this technology is a little less like an Iron Man suit and more like a giant ant suit, but we're definitely getting there.

Spidey Hands

Ever dream about effortlessly scaling the Empire State Building to save a dangling damsel in distress à la Peter Parker?

EDISON V. TESLA

Thomas Edison and his one-time-mentee-turned-nemesis, Nikola Tesla, had an ongoing feud over who could sleep less. Tesla often made fun of Edison for being excessively lazy for dozing more than four hours a day.

Well, hold onto your Spiderman action figure. What if we were to tell you that today you could do just that…only very slowly and while making a lot of noise?

Engineering students from Utah State University accepted a challenge posed by the US Army to create a device that could get four Special Forces soldiers over the wall of a building without the use of grappling hooks. Their solution was a set of vacuum-powered suction cups that can scale just about any building surface. The only problem? The suit literally had two vacuum cleaners attached to the back, making a covert operation possible only if you were assaulting a building filled with working janitors.

It's a Bird, It's a Plane, It's a…Man-Plane Hybrid

Jetpacks have been around since WWII (the Nazis built one called the *Himmelstürmer*, or "sky stormer") and since the day the first one was tested they have pretty much always sucked.

The main problem with the jetpack is that it requires a phenomenal amount of energy (usually highly flammable fuel mounted on your ass) to produce an extremely hard-to-control flight. You really might as well light yourself on fire and jump off a building.

But like so many technological black sheep, this too has its golden sibling: the jet-powered wing suit. This particular best-invention-ever combines a pair of small, kerosene-fueled jet engines with a pair of manageably sized carbon fiber wings worn on the back like the coolest JanSport backpack in the schoolyard. And man, can the sucker fly (well, actually more like fall slowly).

Pilot Yves "Jetman" Rossy has proven the incredible maneuverability of the jet-powered wing suit. He has successfully crossed the Strait of Gibraltar and the English Channel and flown through the Grand Canyon. The suit he uses doesn't have any steering controls, so he drops his shoulders to initiate dives, raises his head to climb, and uses his hands and feet to roll and yaw. Oh, and he can reach a top speed of 190 mph. Unfortunately, you can't just say, "up, up, and away," and launch off the ground; you still need to jump out of an airplane to begin the flight.

Naturally, the wing suit has not gone unnoticed by the military. Germany is developing the Gryphon Glider, a (currently unpowered) six-foot carbon-fiber wing worn by Special Forces paratroopers. With the Gryphon, paratroopers can safely jump out of a transport plane at 30,000 feet in friendly territory and then glide at 130 miles per hour, penetrating enemy lines by up to 120 miles and completely undetected by radar.

Spidergoat Armor

Pound for pound, spider silk is the strongest material in the natural world. Even the smallest spiders can spin webs to catch insects 100 times their size. Some spiders even routinely feed on bats and birds that get caught in their elastic webs. But recently scientists have discovered that the Darwin's bark spider is capable of spinning a web so strong that, when woven together into a lightweight, flexible armor, it would be ten times stronger than Kevlar.

The only issue? When was the last time you heard of a spider farm? Unlike silkworms, arachnids are notoriously difficult to farm, so scientists are attempting to think outside the web…by transferring the spider's silk-producing gene to a universally known domesticated animal: goats. It sounds like something out of a bad science fiction story, but, if successful, newly engineered spidergoats could begin producing super-strong body armor from their udders.

Appendix

SELECTED BIBLIOGRAPHY

Ash, Russell. *Discovering Highwaymen*. New York: Shire, 2011.

Bowden, Mark. *Killing Pablo: The Hunt for the World's Greatest Outlaw*. New York: Grove Atlantic, 2001.

Craughwell, Thomas J. *The Rise and Fall of the Second Largest Empire in History: How Genghis Khan's Mongols Almost Conquered the World*. Beverly, MA: Fair Winds, 2010.

Daniels, Jared. *How to Cook Steak: The 5-Step Formula for the Perfect Steak*. Amazon Kindle.

Diamond, Jared M. *Guns, Germs and Steel: The Fates of Human Societies*. New York: Norton, 1999.

Gorn, Elliott J. *The Manly Art: Bare-Knuckle Prize Fighting in America*. Ithaca, NY: Cornell University, 1951.

Grann, David. *The Lost City of Z: A Tale of Deadly Obsession in the Amazon*. New York: Double Day, 2005.

Hays, J.N. *Epidemics and Pandemics: Their Impacts on Human History*. Santa Barbara, CA: ABC-CLIO, 2005.

Henderson, Charles. *Marine Sniper: 93 Confirmed Kills*. New York: Penguin, 1986.

Heyerdahl, Thor. *Kon-Tiki: Across the Pacific in a Raft*. New York: Simon & Schuster, 1950.

Lendler, Ian. *Alcoholica Esoterica: A Collection of Useful and Useless Information As It Relates to the History and Consumption of All Manner of Booze*. New York: Penguin, 2005.

Martin, Paul S. and Richard G. Klein. *Quaternary Extinctions: A Prehistoric Revolution*. Tucson, AZ: University of Arizona, 1989.

Musashi, Miyamoto and Kenji Tokitsu. *The Complete Book of Five Rings*. Boston: Shambhala, 2000.

Philbrick, Nathaniel. *In the Heart of the Sea: The Tragedy of the Whaleship Essex*. New York: Penguin, 2000.

Protz, Richard. *The Complete Guide to World Beer*. London, U.K.: Carlton, 2004.

Standage, Tom. *A History of the World in 6 Glasses*. New York: Walker, 2005.

Strauss, Darin. *Chang and Eng*. New York: Plume, 2001.

Zacks, Richard. *Island of Vice: Theodore Roosevelt's Quest to Clean Up Sin-Loving New York*. New York: First Anchor, 2012.

 THE MANual

ABOUT THE AUTHORS

Keith Riegert lives in Huntington, New York.

Sam Kaplan resides in Oakland, California.

Each man enjoys a fine glass of whiskey and the company of an intelligent woman.

Made in the USA
Coppell, TX
31 October 2021